The Entrepreneur's Guide to Keeping Your Sh*t Together

The Entrepreneur's Guide to Keeping Your Sh*T Together

How to Run Your Business Without Letting it Run You

Sherry Walling, PhD with Rob Walling

ISBN-13: 9780999651803
ISBN-10: 0999651803

Preview

H ey there! Thanks for checking out our new book. We hope you love it! Much of what we're sharing in the book originally showed up on our weekly podcast. You can find it at ZenFounder.com. While you're there, sign up for our mailing list and as a thank you, we'll send you a set of exclusive video interviews with several highly successful entrepreneurs sharing candidly about their battles with depression and the ups and downs of the entrepreneurial life.

Dedications

We dedicate this book to our kids. We hope that each one of you will come to know the ultimate entrepreneurial success: the crafting of a life rich in freedom, creativity, adventure, meaning, and love.

We also dedicate this book to our friends. Thank you for helping us to keep *our* sh*t together. Without you, this book wouldn't have been possible. And we wouldn't have wanted to write it anyway.

Table of Contents

A Note

The entrepreneurial world is composed of lots of different kinds of folks. Throughout this book, we did our best to use examples, and language, that is inclusive of the many diverse individuals who identify as entrepreneurs. To this end, we alternated male and female pronouns with each chapter. We're always talking about men and women, but the he/she, her/him use of both pronouns gets laborious to read.

Similarly, we used the word "business" to encompass the many different creative and technical pursuits that entrepreneurs have. Perhaps you are an author writing a book, or a coder developing software, or an artist creating beautiful paintings to hang on the walls of our homes. These are all businesses in their own right, and we hope that you can substitute the word business in this book for whatever it is that you have worked so hard to create.

Introduction

We couldn't solve the problem of shared custody. I wanted to take the job in Connecticut. He wanted to return to California. We both wanted to have plenty of time with our 18-month-old son.

Our story started out so perfectly.

We met on the track team at the University of California, Davis. Rob watched me walk across the field one fall day and "just happened" to overhear my conversation with the coach about having to take calculus during afternoon training. Ever the entrepreneur, Rob graciously volunteered to run with me in the mornings.

We spent hours running in circles, chatting, teasing, competing, and eventually coming to know each other's heartaches and dreams.

Rob's father worked for a large electrical contractor in Silicon Valley, and Rob's life plan—which he had mapped out even as a college student—was to finish his degree and become an executive in that same company. He would start with a degree in electrical engineering and go through a three-year executive apprenticeship with the CEO of the company.

He did it all. Flawlessly.

We began to talk about building a life together, a family, a story of our own.

And that's when we realized that maybe Rob's Silicon Valley dreams were a bit out of our price range. In 1999, $1,400 per month to rent a mobile home in Cupertino, California just didn't seem like the right beginning for two big dreamers fresh out of college.

So Rob turned away from his carefully crafted plan to his other love: coding. We got married and set up house in Sacramento, a much more affordable Californian city. He worked for a start-up, became a consultant, worked for a city government, then worked for another start-up. He maximized on his fantastic combination of a technical mind and interpersonal skills to be an incredibly valued member of whatever team he was playing on. He always had an entrepreneurial side project: a membership website, a real estate dynasty.

Since my husband was doing such a great job of following his dreams, I figured it was about time for me to start following mine: I began a doctoral program in Southern California, working on a PhD in clinical psychology.

After seven years of marriage, we had our son.

People thought I was crazy to become a mother during a doctoral program. I ignored the naysayers because I was so sure that we could handle it. I knew that Rob and I had the energy, the emotional connection, the drive, and the resources we needed.

And actually, for the first year, I was right.

Rob worked from home half-time. I spent the early morning hours writing my dissertation, and two days a week I worked as a training psychologist at a veterans hospital. We carefully controlled our time and had tremendous freedom to organize our lives according to the needs of our little family. We also had a strong network of friends; there were plenty of aunties and uncles who were happy to "borrow" our son for an hour so I could go for a walk or take a yoga class.

And it worked.

Until it didn't.

When my son was about a year old, I was offered a fellowship at Yale University School of Medicine. It was the last step in my doctoral experience and I was lucky enough to land a spot in one of the most prestigious programs in the country. It meant a move and a lifestyle change, but Rob and I were elated at the opportunity. We packed up everything in our little Southern California bungalow and made the trek to the Northeast.

When we arrived, I was delighted. I was so full of energy and hope for my future. Everything seemed to be working out perfectly for my career path, my dreams.

I was happy, but I was stressed. Suddenly, long afternoons at the park were replaced by endless hours behind my computer. And any time Rob and I had previously spent working on our relationship and our family... disappeared.

I have done a lot of self-reflection about what I was feeling at that time in my life. Looking back, I realize that I had a fierce inferiority complex. I was a poor kid from the forests of rural Northern California. I had no academic pedigree, no connections, and no experience operating in the world of grant-funded research. I immersed myself in my work with the ferocity of someone with something to prove.

At the time, I was willing to sacrifice anything to reach my career goals.

And in retrospect, I very nearly sacrificed everything.

My family. My marriage. My relationship with my child. And, of course, my emotional health.

Just as I was ramping up my work to a record level, Rob was growing increasingly tired of working for consulting clients.

He had read The 4-Hour Workweek by Timothy Ferriss and began to dream about a different way of working and living. He began to blog. He took on only the most lucrative consulting gigs so that he could build a financial arsenal to do something called "products."

I didn't really understand what he was doing or thinking, but to be honest, I'm not sure how well I was listening.

This disconnect quickly drove a wedge between us.

To an outsider, we looked like the perfect picture of young talent—we had the education, the collective abilities, and the potential to really do something with our lives.

We appeared to have it all together, but it all started to unravel sometime in November 2007. Just as the first cold front came in, the heat in our tiny Connecticut apartment went out. We bundled the baby under layers of sweaters and puffer jackets as we fought with the landlord over our rental contract. Our days became a constant battle of who did what, who said what, and who was going to figure out how to pay for what.

And as if that wasn't enough, I spent those cold winter months flying from the East Coast to the West Coast enduring grueling two-day interviews for tenure-track faculty jobs.

And then my grandpa died.

I was tired.

I was emotionally drained.

There weren't enough hours in the day. In the *year*, for that matter.

But there also wasn't any chance I could back down, take a break, or rest.

As a doctoral candidate in clinical psychology, I knew what I needed: sleep, quiet, and time spent meaningfully connected with the people that I loved. I needed to rest my frantic mind and engage with my work from a more focused, grounded place.

But as I now understand after years of working with therapy and consulting clients… knowing and doing are different phenomena.

My research fellowship at Yale was ripe with opportunities and I wanted to make the most of them as I launched the prestigious academic career I'd always wanted. There were endless seminars and writing opportunities, and mountains of papers to read. There were networking events, guest lectures from field leaders, and study sessions.

There was enough work to keep me busy for a hundred hours each week.

The only down time I could afford were the moments I gave to my little boy.

I didn't feel like I had time for my husband.

Secretly, we were lonely, resentful, and very tired people. Neither of us felt understood or cared about. Neither of us felt supported. Our jobs consumed all of our time. All of our emotional energy went to our son.

We came very close that winter to shutting down our life together, and had we been able to agree on custody, we may just well have lost everything. But, for the sake of our son, we decided to give it one more try.

I turned down a postdoctoral fellowship at Yale and, instead, we moved to Boston for yet another new beginning.

You may know some of what came after for Rob and me: several successful start-ups, MicroConf, a couple of podcasts, a PhD, and another child.

Had we given up and gotten divorced at that time when our lives were imploding, it would have been a great tragedy. We are well suited to each other, and our partnership has allowed us to accomplish more together than we could have possibly done individually.

But it took work. Lots of work. And lots of tough choices.

By now, Rob and I have spent years trying to figure out what we consider the ultimate question for business owners and entrepreneurs: How can you do the best, most meaningful work *and* have a life that you love at the same time?

That question—and the many answers we have to it—are contained in the pages of this book. This book started to take shape in my mind during that cold, dark Connecticut winter and then came to fruition over the years as I emerged from that dark time in my life. That season of our lives epitomizes the problems this book attempts to steer you away from. We were disconnected, burned-out people who were longing for a more creative, productive, joyful life.

This book explains how to be an entrepreneur and be holistically healthy, productive, and connected. (Yes, it's possible!)

It's about being successful with your business, *and* with your relationships.

It's about being an integrated person—someone who thrives in work and "life."

It's about learning to listen to yourself; learning to trust your own wisdom.

It's about facing the hard parts of the entrepreneurial life.

It's about problem-solving, coping, and managing the monsters in your mind.

It's about giving yourself permission to craft the life that you want.

This book is for entrepreneurs and their significant others. We broadly define entrepreneurs as people responsible for—or those who wish to be responsible for—their own paycheck, their own livelihood. Perhaps you own a software company, a WordPress plugin, or a productized consulting company. Maybe you are a freelance writer or designer. Or you've raised a round of funding to start a high-growth start-up. Perhaps you own a boutique law firm or sell organic lotion on Amazon. The content of the business is not as important as what it means to be responsible for running a little piece of the economy. Your piece. Or what it means to be running a little piece of life. Your life.

Whether you've built, or are striving to build, a business that allows you to be in control of your life… you will run into moments like we did back in 2007. Our hope is that this book prepares you for them so that the story of your life is happy, healthy, and successful.

Here's to living better stories.

1

The Entrepreneur's Dilemma

Every once in a while, Rob or I will succumb to what we affectionately call "founder's panic."

You've been there, too, haven't you?

Questions start rolling around in your mind, making you doubt everything you've accomplished so far and everything you dream of doing in the future. What if Google changes its algorithm again? What if a new business comes along and makes us obsolete? What if my awesome support guy quits? What if growth stagnates? What if we have to dip into personal savings? What if we *lose* our personal savings? What *if*?

The waterfall of questions is accompanied by the commiserative shallow breathing, wild-eyed stare, and tightening throat that all so commonly signal angst.

In the midst of a worrisome season, a friend asked Rob why he didn't just return to the stability of salaried employment. That was the perfect question to help us shake the funk and dig right back into our entrepreneurial dreams.

Being entrepreneurs is so at the core of who we are that even the mention of trading our angst for the ease of a salaried gig reminds us about everything that is right with the entrepreneur life. We love our freedom. We love organizing our days around what our family needs. We love to work from different places. We love designing our work lives around interesting tasks and important problems. We love building things. We love the challenge of signing our own paychecks. We love the ability to choose how much or how little we want to work during a given day, month, or season of our lives.

Even with all of the stress, the hustle, the occasional panic, the at-times financial instability, and the worry, Rob and I are undoubtedly happier and more fulfilled as entrepreneurs.

It's just who we are.

Throughout the next several chapters, I'm going to walk you through the whys and hows of being a successful entrepreneur—a person who thinks big, executes, and is willing to take responsibility for making sure their dreams are reached. But that's not all we're going to talk about—because, let's be honest, you've probably already read a hundred books just like that. I'm going to use my background in clinical psychology to show you how you can be an entrepreneur *and* stay sane and emotionally healthy through the stress, the ups and downs, and the many successes and failures that come with the entrepreneur life.

I assure you, it's possible. I'm going to give you loads of tips, tactics, and ideas that will help you make small adjustments to the thinking patterns you use to approach business and life. These small adjustments may seem minuscule, but I promise that they can be extremely impactful on your mental health *and* the health of your business.

The reality is that without a healthy founder, it is impossible to have a healthy business. To fully enjoy the freedom of the entrepreneurial life, a founder must take responsibility for the balancing act that places the well-being of the self at the center.

So while it may seem like an extraneous thing to focus on when you have code to write, production costs and prototypes, office space and outlines, or storyboards and business plans to work on, your mental health is an essential first step. There's no way around it.

It's the foundation upon which you can build your business and your life.

FREEDOM, INGENUITY, ADVENTURE, AND MEANING

To borrow a phrase from author Simon Sinek, it is imperative that any book on founder psychology *starts with why*. The way one answers the question of why shapes everything else. Why do this? Why choose the entrepreneurial life? Why leave a high-paying consulting gig? Why not pursue a high-salaried journey up a corporate ladder? Why not choose a job that you can easily explain at the dinner table? Why not a 9-to-5 job with 2.5 kids living in an energy-efficient house in the suburbs with black shutters and a white picket fence and a dog?

The answer is values. Our decisions are shaped by what we value.

Specifically, Rob and I have some shared, core values that directly led us into entrepreneurship: *freedom, ingenuity, adventure,* and *meaning.* These values are deeply held parts of our personalities and have shaped how we see and interact with the world.

These values are what give us our drive, our passion, and our power to persevere.

They have become our "meta-goals," the filter that we use to determine how we confront life-shaping choices. And I'm going to go out on a limb and guess that many entrepreneurs share these values with us.

And these values are what make it impossible for some of us to settle for the conventional expectations that others might have for us.

For an entrepreneur, the drive to live in a free, self-actualized, autonomous way outweighs all of the trappings of the alternatives. Entrepreneurs can't help but be entrepreneurs: They want to create, to risk, to build. The question of why is central because the challenges are so immense. Most start-ups fail. There's the time, the work, and the sacrifice. It is entirely possible that your work will not yield that leisurely lifestyle business or that big exit. Failure is a very real possibility, perhaps the most likely possibility.

Even if failure is not the outcome, there is a high price to pay in sleepless nights, long days, and the stress-induced breakdown of the body. It is easy to drift into an existence marked by anxiety and isolation.

So why do we do it?

Because we value freedom, ingenuity, adventure, and meaning.

And we're willing to sacrifice a lot in order to cling to the values that we hold dear.

Freedom

Man is condemned to be free; because once thrown into the world, he is responsible for everything he does.

—JEAN-PAUL SARTRE

As all Spider-Man fans know, "with great power comes great responsibility." The entrepreneur's superpower is her freedom. She can craft her tasks, choose her location, design her schedule, and hand-pick her team. She signs her own paycheck.

Entrepreneurs want freedom over their time, to-do list, goals, and location. They aren't willing to spend 40 (or 50 or 60) hours every week sitting in a cubicle, staring at fabric-covered walls while doing tasks assigned by someone else. They aren't willing to do things just because that's the way they have always been done—they want the freedom to use the full power of their brain to create new and better solutions to old problems, to make the world more productive, more efficient, and better. They aren't willing to settle for punching the clock day in and day out, for doing a job and collecting a paycheck.

I think anyone reading these words would agree that the freedom to work when you want, to play when you want, to create, to innovate, to make lots of choices about your work life, sounds pretty amazing. Until you think about the risk. The trade-off for this freedom is instability. When you trade in your 9-to-5 job for the freedom of a founder, you can no longer count on a paycheck being direct-deposited into your bank account on the first day of every month. You can no longer walk away from your desk for a long weekend and figure that the person in the next cubicle will finish the work.

The existence of risk leads to the question that is an age-old philosophical exercise, the existential dilemma: Can one have so much freedom that it creates such a weight of responsibility that one is no longer free? I think so. With all that freedom comes a lot of responsibility. And I think that finding a way to balance the freedom that an entrepreneur craves with the responsibility that is required to get that freedom is the key to staying healthy and sane as an entrepreneur.

An example of this balance happened in 2008 as Rob was transitioning from consulting to products. His *number* (the amount of money he needed to make each month to cover our expenses) was around $8,000. He had just left consulting—where he was making 2 to 2.5 times that amount each month—and he had cobbled together a small portfolio of products that were, in most months, hitting his number.

Even though he had never experienced so much freedom, he was constantly worried about hitting that number. So much so that he felt guilty any time he wasn't either working or thinking about work. The struggle was that he wasn't being paid by the hour any longer (the double-edged sword of product income not being tied to hours worked), so all that extra work never added up to extra money in his paycheck. He could have done whatever he wanted with his days. But he wouldn't let himself exercise this freedom.

It took him three or four months to work through this feeling and begin to fully enjoy his newfound (and hard-earned) freedom, including months where he sold things on eBay and Craigslist to make up for shortfalls. But after a few months of realizing that the number was just that—a number—and that the true freedom he valued came from allowing himself the freedom to miss the number, he was able to step back and really grow his portfolio and his business in a way that aligned with his value of freedom.

Ingenuity

> The true sign of intelligence is not knowledge but imagination.
>
> — **ALBERT EINSTEIN**

Entrepreneurs are ingenious, creative people. They thrive on finding novel answers to problems. They want to do things differently, ask different kinds of questions, and create new solutions. They are willing to trade a predictable task list for one that they generate themselves.

This ingenuity is a great thing.

Imagine our world without the ingenious creativity of entrepreneurs.

No Teslas to get you over the bridge to the concert. (No minivans, either, for that matter.) No MacBook Pro. No Facebook, Instagram, or Twitter. No Snapchat (okay, so maybe that wouldn't be that life-altering). No special sleeve that keeps your halved avocado from going brown. No iPhone X. No wetsuits for surfing in chilly Northern California waters. No tiny spinning devices that distract you when you're feeling stressed so that you can refocus. And no electricity, not to mention no indoor plumbing.

Our modern world is built on the dreams of entrepreneurs.

Ingenuity is what drives inventors to invent things and entrepreneurs to stay up until 3 a.m. staring at a business plan, thinking that maybe, yes maybe, it could just work.

What I enjoy most about being an entrepreneur is the exact same thing I used to enjoy the least: having to come up with solutions out of thin air.

This freedom is daunting at first, as there is no longer a teacher to tell you where you should color, a boss to tell you what to work on, or a client to describe what they are looking for. But learning to cope with the need to constantly tackle difficult problems, with incomplete information, and come up with a reasonable game plan, is what makes this work interesting. Once you have the freedom to think creatively and solve hard problems, you can't go back.

When I see someone with founder traits who is slogging away in a stifling 9-to-5 job, I believe the world is worse off. Ingenuity is one of the optimal uses of an entrepreneur's mind, and it's one of the core values of every founder I know. They value the ability to create, to stretch, to grow, to think way outside the box, and to push beyond the boundaries of our current technology. This ingenuity drives us—and it also drives greatness.

Adventure

> *The purpose of life is to live it, to taste experience to the utmost, to reach out eagerly and without fear for newer and richer experience.*

> — **Eleanor Roosevelt**

Another core value of the entrepreneur is an orientation toward adventure. We've already established that the founder life involves an element of risk. And while that risk could be daunting for many, for an entrepreneur it is invigorating. It's what drives us and causes us to dig in and work harder, to push the envelope, to go the distance.

Entrepreneurs are willing to take risks in order to stake out a new path, even if there is a chance it may fail.

After five years in a doctoral program and two years of doing research fellowships at Yale and the National Center for Posttraumatic Stress Disorder, I was well qualified for a highly coveted position as a university professor. And so that's what I did: For three years, I was a full-time professor. Unfortunately, it wasn't a job I loved. Committees, hierarchy, contentious relationships between faculty and administration, forms, procedures, bureaucracy, an occasional disengaged and entitled student... I was miserable.

Leaving the job I'd spent so many years preparing for was one of the most difficult decisions of my life. It echoed the unique mixture of excitement, anxiety, and mustered courage I'd experienced 13 years earlier when I drained my savings account to purchase a plane ticket to Ghana in West Africa. For a year. First trip out of the country. I was 19.

This willingness to step away from a career trajectory or get on a plane for an unknown adventure has been my superpower as an entrepreneur and as an entrepreneur's spouse. I would rather cultivate courage than settle for boredom. I would rather risk the wild than live in a comfortable cage.

My year in Ghana taught me that there are hundreds of thousands of ways to live. Walking away from an academic career taught me that there are no shortcuts to a satisfying life. I can plan well, but I won't know the outcome until I arrive. I also learned that the story of my life doesn't end until my last breath. I have learned to love a good venture into the wild unknown.

Meaning

> Life has no meaning a priori... It is up to you to give it a meaning, and value is nothing but the meaning that you choose.

— JEAN-PAUL SARTRE

Perhaps the most foundational value is the drive toward crafting a meaningful life. Ultimately, entrepreneurs want to pursue problems, activities, and goals that they find meaningful. They don't want to generate energy for someone else's agenda. They are willing to take full existential responsibility for their lives.

Despite the freedom, or possibly because of the freedom, the entrepreneur's life is a heavy burden to bear. An entrepreneur is the heart and soul of her business. The business works because she works. The bottom line can be affected by the entrepreneur's mood on a given day, by her level of sleep, or by how much she drank the night before. Creativity, intellect, motivation, and patience drive how much a venture is thriving or falling apart. Without the person of the entrepreneur, the business is nothing. There's nothing to pitch, invoice, code or stabilize. The entrepreneurial life involves intense pressure.

But inside of this intense pressure is our final core value: the quest for meaning.

For an entrepreneur, her entire livelihood, business, future depends on one thing: putting herself "out there." An entrepreneur, in her quest for meaning, must be willing to put her name and signature on something that she has done. Maybe it's an invention. Perhaps it's an idea. It's quite possibly a business plan or a shop or a new technology. Sometimes it's a book or a piece of art. Whatever it is, the entrepreneur doesn't just create, but she creates for the public sphere. She puts her work, her ideas, her creativity, her future up on display for the whole world to see.

Obviously, the long-term viability of any business or brand means that the founder has to put herself out there. She creates something from her heart and mind and then releases it into the world. This action is inherently motivating. Naturally, the potential for reward is there: If the idea or business or brand is successful, the entrepreneur's life dreams are fulfilled.

But it is also inherently scary.

Because in order to be successful, an entrepreneur must push something out there that means something. The business, idea, or product is part of them, part of their passion, their heart, their soul. It must be personal and real. Which means that any successes and any failures are also personal and real.

And when you do things in public, you set yourself up for criticism.

A few years ago, I did a talk on founder psychology at a conference we had in Barcelona. The talk went pretty well—I really felt like I delivered some great tips for, and gave insight into, the psychology behind entrepreneurship. Which is why I was so surprised when a man came up to me at the hotel the next morning while I was eating breakfast with my sons and told me that he thought my talk dragged on and was boring.

It stung.

As I poured my son's milk on his cereal, my mind started to race. Was my talk really boring? Did that entire room of people feel like I had nothing to offer other than a snoozefest? Was everyone else judging me as well? Should I just stop doing public speaking and go back to doing something else that I'm probably better at?

But I stopped myself.

I grabbed myself a croissant and intentionally switched my thinking. I thought about all of the people who had complimented my talk after it was over (there were many), and how several people had emailed me requesting more information (hence this book), and how there had been lines of people waiting to talk to me and ask me questions. I also thought about the entrepreneurs who have told me about their struggles with loneliness, depression, suicidal thoughts, facing a breakup with their co-founder, being on the brink of divorce, or the impulsive decisions that have cost hundreds of thousands of dollars.

The bottom line is that I believe my work is meaningful. I was on that stage because I believed that I had something helpful to say. Maybe not to everyone, but at least to a few people. I can work on my stage presence and talk structure, but those are secondary. They are the wrapping of the package; the meaning is the core.

We're going to talk about how to handle criticism and failure much more in the coming chapters, but for now, I want to point out that the quest for meaning can often be the fuel that helps us do hard things. If I were on that stage purely for myself, I would crumble under criticism. But because I believe that the work exists for a purpose bigger than myself, I find the power to fight my tendency to run from negative feedback.

Meaning it should motivate you to get out there, to watch the growth curve happen, to think creatively, to invent, and to dream. It should inspire you to level up, both in the quantity of your work and in the quality. It should help you to gain confidence and gain experience.

Allow your quest for meaning to become the driver in your business, and I promise that you will see change. I've reached the point now that I often think, "I can't believe I was ever scared of a conference talk!" I've done it so many times that the meaning outweighs the risk. I'm also increasingly okay with the fact that my talks aren't going to "land" for everyone. I'm there for the 5, 10, 50, 189 people that need to hear what I have to say. It's personally gratifying to not be afraid, to pursue the goal without being nervous. As entrepreneurs, the driver that causes us to wake up each day ready to work, that moves the needle through our businesses, is where we find the meaning we are looking for.

HOW FREEDOM, INGENUITY, ADVENTURE, AND MEANING AFFECT YOUR MENTAL HEALTH

There's a catch.

The core values that most entrepreneurs share—freedom, ingenuity, adventure, and meaning—come with baggage. This is because with freedom comes a huge dose of anxiety. With ingenuity comes opportunity for failure. Those of us who handwrite the scripts of our lives create adventure, but we can also find ourselves in unknown, unpredictable, and unstable surroundings. And in the quest for meaning, entrepreneurs often find themselves feeling isolated and alone.

Freedom and anxiety.

Ingenuity and failure.

Adventure and instability.

Meaning and isolation.

These stand in stark contrast to each other and represent the great risk of being an entrepreneur. In order for me to address the mental health of entrepreneurs, I have to talk about the many risks that come with the entrepreneurial life. I would be remiss if I didn't tell the truth about the shadowy side of this lifestyle that makes founders vulnerable to physical health problems, relationship problems, and mental health problems.

I believe that the first step to finding a solution to a problem is to spell it out. Name it. And then figure out how to solve that problem one step at a time.

So I'll spell it out: Being an entrepreneur is brutal on your mental health. It's ripe with anxiety and instability; many entrepreneurs fail time and time again and, yes, in doing so, they feel isolated and meaningless. It's hard.

Which means that as an entrepreneur, you have to get serious about self-responsibility, self-mastery, and self-care. Each of us carries the weight of the freedom that we have. For many of us, this means anxiety, loneliness, hours of effort without reward or recognition, late nights, early mornings, and sometimes the sacrifice of the relationships, hobbies, and values that we hold dear.

Don't get me wrong, most days I wouldn't choose another path for Rob or myself, or for our family. But if we don't take a hard look at the shadows, at what the dark side is, we can easily be trapped in the "condemned" part of our freedom. I believe that it is essential to tell the truth about the challenges of the path we have chosen. It is only then that we have the chance to maximize the benefits of our freedom without falling too deeply into the condemnations of our responsibilities.

We experience the "condemnation" from our freedom through anxiety, isolation, instability, and failure.

People who struggle with anxiety, instability, isolation, and failure often experience major issues with their physical health. Many physiological illnesses are driven, if not caused, by anxiety, instability, isolation, and failure. Additionally, people who are experiencing anxiety, instability, isolation, and failure often act in ways that lead to the dissolution of relationships. Marriages are destroyed. Friendships are ruined. Relationships between children and parents are broken.

Can you see why these are such important things for us as entrepreneurs to address? Here is a bit more about each of these issues and how you as an entrepreneur can address them in your life.

Anxiety and instability

Even the most cool, calm, and collected person in the universe might have a swirling storm inside as she faces the fears of her own future and the personal liabilities that come with it. But let's be honest: Entrepreneurs aren't the most cool, calm, and collected people in the universe. Far from it. Which means that while the ordinary person may struggle with anxiety from time to time, founders are often burdened by bouts of anxiety that keep them up at night and become a threat to their emotional health.

Anxiety lives in your mind.

It is driven by instabilities and unknowns. Shifts in revenue, conversions, an unidentifiable bug in the code. A competitor with a slightly better product. It keeps your mind swirling at 2 a.m. with "what ifs" and "hows" and "maybes." And for some (many, even), it creates panic attacks.

People literally feel like they can't breathe, and are sweaty with a pounding pulse because the anxiety they are feeling is almost crushing. Sadly, when we talk to entrepreneurs, it's apparent these reactions are somewhat common.

It's commonplace, yes, but when anxiety is elevated for long periods of time, it can affect your sleep, your ability to perform during the day, and your relationships. Your body tries to react to the activation of these really big and heavy bouts of stress with tense muscles that won't relax, with digestion problems that don't go away, and with headaches that seem to go on and on for days.

This is the point at which we begin to make bad decisions. It's when we as entrepreneurs begin to long for escape, to find something in life that will relieve the pressure, the pain. It is when founders leave their businesses and dreams. It may begin with some not-so-great options like drinking that 5th, 6th, 7th glass of scotch. Or crossing the line and yelling at people. Or saying mean things to your spouse. Or being super edgy with your children. Or insulting your co-workers. Or being sassy or snappy with a client.

Anxiety can lead to really bad behavior.

We'll talk much more about this in later chapters and you'll quickly see that the trigger for many of the problem-causing behaviors for entrepreneurs stems from a sense of anxiety that's driven by instability.

Isolation

Do you feel isolated?

Before you answer, I want you to consider a few things. Perhaps you are just starting out and do most of your work alone somewhere in a converted closet in the back of your house. But more likely than not, you have a team—a group of people who are helping you to build your business or your dream. It may be your family and friends, or a team you hired. And so your gut response to my question may be that of course you're not isolated. You have people.

But let me ask again: Do you *feel* isolated?

Many entrepreneurs feel isolated not because they are actually alone in the world, but instead because they have an innate sense that they are the one who alone carries the burden of their work. No one else knows as much. No one else cares as much. No one else has as much to lose. No one else has as much to prove. When you think about it that way, I'm guessing you probably start nodding your head. Because most—if not all—entrepreneurs feel isolated at one point or another.

Being a founder is a lonely path. And if you are introverted like me, you may think that sounds like a good thing. When we were just starting out, I remember telling Rob that I loved the fact that as a founder, I would be able to avoid dealing with people and, thus, be able to be alone with my thoughts and work more effectively. Which sounds good at first, until you realize that everything is riding on your work.

It's perfectly okay to be a Lone Wolf or to work independently, but when we lose deep connection with others, our health suffers and our businesses suffer. As an entrepreneur, one of the smartest things you can do is to make sure you are in a community—not only with your family and friends, but also in a community with other entrepreneurs. I recommend finding ways to connect with other founders—perhaps through a mastermind group or a conference community, or even an online forum—so that you can build relationships and camaraderie with those who understand what it's like to be an entrepreneur. (If you want to look ahead, we talk more about this in Chapter 10.)

Building relationships will do more than help to break a sense of personal isolation.

It will help your business to thrive.

Failure

The final thing that we as entrepreneurs have to cope with a little bit differently compared to the rest of the world is the very real possibility of failure.

In 2014, Rob almost tanked his business. His email marketing start-up, Drip, was not growing as fast as he would have liked, so he decided to hire three developers to accelerate the pace of the product launch. But, due to a series of small mismanagements, he found himself with less than 45 days of payroll in the bank, and nowhere near enough revenue to cover it once the bank account was empty.

It felt like an ending, like a failure.

He was devastated. He had worked so hard for so long, starting as an electrician doing hourly work, moving to a low-end office job on a construction site, then moving into a salaried programmer role, then to consulting and, finally, to products… and it was all about to go down the drain because he placed a bet on an idea that wasn't panning out.

When he talks about this time, Rob often tells me that he has few regrets in his life, but one of them is the distraction and stress he put us all through as Drip was failing. During that time, he worked too much and stressed even more. He made big sacrifices in order to pay the bills. It's a time that we both remember with great angst—and I would never wish that on any founder.

One of the hardest parts of being an entrepreneur is that no matter how much you achieve, the threat of failure is always looming. The reality is that you are going to put yourself out there and the client may not like your work. Even more, I can all but guarantee that you are going to fail on some level at some point, and at that point, it is only going to be you that you have to blame. You that bears the responsibility for cleaning up the mess.

That's a tough fact to wrap your head around.

Sadly, it is likely that when that inevitable failure comes, you will fill your head with untruths like "I'm just not capable of this" or "Maybe I shouldn't be doing this" or "Maybe I should go back and work for someone else."

At that moment, you have a choice. Do you press in, address the negative thought patterns and find ways to deal with them so you can move forward? Or do you listen to them?

You need to have a really serious talk with yourself about how you deal with inevitable failure. Be open to the fact that it's part of the gig and find a way not to be afraid of it. Have a plan for how you're going to deal with it, and cope with it and don't run from it. The heavy, serious warning for all founders is that we're fallible—you may feel like Superman or Wonder Woman—but you are a vulnerable person who has a lot riding on your dreams. You can be broken, and when you are, it will hurt worse than failure does for a regular Jane whose heart and soul isn't tied into her work.

Keeping your core values—freedom, ingenuity, adventure, and meaning—in the forefront of your mind, even when you face failure, is one of the best tools you have to combat the challenges of the entrepreneur life. Returning to "why" can be a steady reminder of why the entire struggle is worth it. There will be good days, and there will be lots of bad days. The question is whether or not you have the life that you want.

We'll talk much more about this later in the book, but for now, I'll leave you with this: It's okay for you to have a connection with your own vulnerability. It's essential for you to have a connection to your own values.

2

Understanding where you Came from
to Optimize where you're Going

Is an entrepreneur born or made?

It seems like a silly question, considering the fact that the very essence of being an entrepreneur involves that gritty, self-made spirit that makes entrepreneurs great. Every single business, invention, technology, book, or concept started as an idea from someone who was willing to take that idea and grow it into something meaningful. Something big and real.

But what if that self-made, self-starting, entrepreneurial spirit is something more than a learned behavior? What if it begins with innate personality traits, nurtured in a way that leads to the perfect mix of creativity and grit? What if it is a rebellion? Or a reaction against a painful experience? What if the entrepreneurial spirit is a result of natural ambition mixed with genius and hard work?

When I entered the field of psychology, I felt certain that I wouldn't waste time on antiquated explorations of someone's relationship with his mother. I was sure that health and wellness would be a function of present-oriented and practical problem-solving. I figured that old Freudian ideas about the importance of early life experiences were simply remnants of old-fashioned, Victorian-era medicine and something that wouldn't affect my work.

I wasn't entirely wrong about the value of the present-focus. No one who focuses on their past while neglecting their current needs is able to move forward. However, I admit, I was really wrong about how important a person's early life experiences and relationships are. Our grown-up, professional selves are solidly rooted in who we've been since the beginning of our lives.

Interestingly, the impact of a person's past is even more important for someone who is an entrepreneur. Unlike an employee, you are intimately tied to the success of your business. Your identity, your personal life, and your history are all integral components that will determine the success of your business. Your past shapes how you handle risk, disappointment, success, fear, relationships, and conflict.

To put it simply: Even with all of your self-made, self-starting spirit and grit, the shadows of your past are shaping—and will continue to shape—the success of your business.

We all like to believe that we are completely in charge of our lives. We want to be able to live in this moment and be free to make of it what we want. While there is certainly some truth to that, the reality is that this moment is an accumulation of all of our other moments and we cannot exist independently of our past. Personal success depends on our own ability to wield the strengths and weaknesses that we've downloaded from our pasts.

So how does this affect you as an entrepreneur? If your past goes unchecked, it can be a script that you blindly live out, a factor that changes your business without you even realizing it. Likewise, if you carefully study your past—your upbringing, your natural tendencies, and your innate personality traits—you will become armed with a new arsenal of tools that will lead to greater success.

IS FOCUSING ON THE PAST A WASTE OF TIME?

At first glance, you may feel the way I once did: Focusing on the past wastes precious time that could be spent growing your business. So is it really worth it?

I think so. There is a substantial body of high-quality research supporting the primary importance of understanding our past. Anyone who thinks the past doesn't matter... well, you're wrong. Sorry, you're just wrong. As a discipline, psychology has come a long way since Freud, but the basic tenets of developmental neuroscience, epigenetics, and other rapidly emerging fields support his assertion that what happens to you as a kid matters very much to the development of who you become as an adult.

Without giving you a dissertation on epigenetics, telomeres, and the size and structure of the hippocampus, amygdala, and prefrontal cortex, I want to simply say that there is tremendous scientific evidence that our personal pasts greatly influence our values, our personalities, our relationships, and our lives.

One of the most striking pieces of evidence that the past matters comes from a study done in the late 1990s when the Centers for Disease Control and Prevention partnered with Kaiser Permanente to conduct the Adverse Childhood Experiences Study. They assessed over 17,000 people and reviewed their medical records. They asked people about their exposure to 10 different categories of early life adversity: physical, sexual, and psychological abuse; family violence; a mentally ill caregiver; an incarcerated parent; an addicted parent; physical neglect; emotional neglect; and parental divorce.

What they discovered is revolutionizing the field of health care.

This 10-question survey about childhood may be the best tool we have for predicting adulthood health care utilization. Based on people's answers, researchers were able to predict heart disease, obesity, substance abuse, depression, and suicide among many other things. Interesting, right? If you want to read more about this study, you can find the whole thing here: https://www.cdc.gov/violenceprevention/acestudy/about.html

What's more, people who experienced four or more of the childhood adversity categories were seven (yes, seven!) times more likely to identify as an alcoholic, twice as likely to be diagnosed with heart disease or cancer, and 460% more likely to suffer from depression than people who never experienced adverse situations as children. Additionally, the lifespan of people who had experienced six or more categories of childhood adversity was more than 20 years shorter than that of their peers.

So what does that all mean for you as an entrepreneur? If you had a tough childhood, does it mean you're destined to fail? And do those lucky children who had everything perfect when they were little have a free pass to a successful business?

Not exactly.

Traumatic experience can change the chemistry and physiology of our brains. But it isn't childhood trauma alone that leads to major health issues and early death. The negative feelings and emotions from adverse experiences can lead to unhealthy behaviors that break down the body and the mind. To put it simply, people who have unresolved issues from their past may find it more difficult to soothe and regulate their emotions, and may fall into unhealthy behavior patterns like excessive drinking, impulsive spending, drug use, overeating, lack of exercise, or self-sabotaging and making other self-destructive choices.

Life is not a path set in concrete. There are ways to mitigate the damaging effects of early life adversity. There are ways to unlock the secret strengths that are present in even the most traumatic early life. We have some choice about how we let the past influence our present decisions and future well-being. But it is difficult to make proactive, informed choices if we don't take the time to consider the personal stories that are shaping who we are.

WHAT MAKES AN ENTREPRENEUR AN ENTREPRENEUR?

As an entrepreneur, your past not only affects who you are, but because your business is inherently tied to who you are, the success of your business is also affected by your past.

As humans, we tell stories to transform ourselves, to learn about our history, and potentially transcend our experiences. We tell stories to make a difference in our world, to broaden our perspective to see further than normal, and to act beyond a story that may have imprisoned or enslaved us.

Marshall Duke, a professor at Emory University, studies families. He found that families that tell their own stories—the time your grandfather set the barn on fire, the day you were born, the day your father lost his job, the day your mother took you to see your favorite movie three times in a row—are the families that are the happiest and the most resilient when tragedy happens.

My hunch is that the same is true for companies and for entrepreneurs. The success of your start-up is largely dependent on how well you handle the events that happen in the life of your business—the stories that compose the history of your business. Being a founder is not a job; it is an identity. Your success depends in part on how you understand your own story and your role in the story of your business.

When your app is having a bad month, when free trials are not converting to sign-ups, and when you haven't sold a single product in a week, it is helpful to remember the story of when you were 15 years old and trying to build your first webpage. It sucked. Or the time the servers went down and your entire team stayed up all night. You tried and you tried, and you were so frustrated because nothing seemed to work. It also helps to remember that you didn't stay there. That moment passed.

You learned, you grew.

But the story shapes how you are going to respond to your future business struggles and marketing woes. You can repeat the story if it had a good outcome, or you have the power to try for a different ending. From the mission, culture, or efficiency of your company to the decisions that shape your family and your personal life, these stories are going to be the threads that carry you through difficult days and the inspiration that moves you toward success.

Good story, bad story, sad story. Whatever your story is, it played a huge role in helping you become the person you are right now. A story of trauma and loss tells you how much you've survived. A story of love and support tells you how much you're valued. A story of struggles in school or a sports injury tells you how much you have overcome. A story of successful parents teaches you how to achieve. A story of poverty teaches you how to do more with less. A story of loss shows you how important connections are. The story of your spelling bee win teaches you how to diligently work toward a goal. The story of your playoff loss tells you how it feels to fail one day and wake up for school the next day.

My interest in how the past shapes the present was the impetus for the Founder Origin Stories Project. For this project, I conducted in-depth interviews with entrepreneurs from a variety of backgrounds to try to piece together the many factors that make an entrepreneur an entrepreneur. (You can hear these interviews as well as my analysis at ZenFounder.com if you are interested.) Not surprisingly, I found several themes that made me realize that there are certain personality traits, childhood events, and values that entrepreneurs share:

1) Early adversity (with lots of support)

None of the entrepreneurs that I interviewed had picture-perfect, rainbows-and-butterflies childhoods. Instead, most of them had significant adversity that occurred during their childhood years. Several entrepreneurs lost parents in elementary school. Others experienced significant struggles with anxiety, isolation, or disability. A few had early run-ins with the law. Most had difficulty conforming to a traditional school environment. Several founders talked about violence and poverty in their early lives.

There is a difference, however, between these successful entrepreneurs and many others: The successful entrepreneurs had tools, support systems, and strategies that allowed them to weather these difficulties well. Most of the time, there was at least one loving parent or supportive teacher who seemed to see them for who they were. Every one of the successful entrepreneurs that I interviewed described feeling loved and supported in the midst of difficulties that they encountered.

There is certainly a body of literature in the psychological research to support this pattern. High adversity with high support leads to perseverance, resilience, and grit. As children, these entrepreneurs learned the ability to encounter hard things without folding. They learned to press into their support systems, to find tools to help them move forward, to persevere even in the midst of difficult circumstances.

2) An inherent need to blaze a trail

The second theme I noticed as I interviewed entrepreneurs is that each one had a clear and consistent need to be a trailblazer. In psychology circles, we might call this "writing a new life schema." For entrepreneurs, the standard models for life don't apply, so they are constantly seeking something more, something different, something better. An entrepreneur isn't going to settle for clocking in at the start of the day and clocking out at 5 p.m. He isn't going to settle for a careful, typical life. He wants more, and is willing to go off the beaten track to find it.

As children, often due to circumstances or their unique innate personality traits and cognitive abilities, young entrepreneurs have to find new ways to define and understand themselves. The default paths laid out before them either don't apply or feel intolerable.

One entrepreneur I interviewed described herself as a "smart, affluent girl with raging ADHD [attention-deficit/hyperactivity disorder]." Because of this quality, she struggled in the typical classroom—labeled as distracted and unfocused. But with the help of her mother and some great teachers, she was moved to a gifted school, and she learned some alternative strategies to get by in school. Instead of sitting while studying, she paced the classroom with note cards in hand. Instead of doing a diorama for her school project, she taught the class a sequential set of movements as part of an onsite lesson. These adaptations to her learning continued as she began to blaze a new trail and started her own successful business. (If you want to hear more about her story, you can listen to it in ZenFounder podcast episode 22.)

Several other entrepreneurs that I interviewed lived between cultures or had multiple cultural identities. For example, Steli Efti grew up as a Greek immigrant in Germany; Hiten Shah was an ethnic Indian born in Africa who immigrated to the U.S.; Ruben Gamez was the son of Mexican and Puerto Rican parents. Each of these people had to blaze trails because their cultural identities didn't fit neatly in one box and "the way things have always been" didn't apply to them. They had to create a little corner in the world in order to find a place for themselves- a place where they could truly be successful.

3) Self-taught, self-led

Another commonality I found between entrepreneurs is that they all have an exemplary ability to be self-taught and self-led. This isn't to say that the entrepreneurs didn't go to school—a number of them have advanced degrees and spent many years taking classes in their area. But entrepreneurs are willing to go beyond formal schooling as they learn. If they see a problem, they figure it out. If they are curious about something, they study it. If they want to know something, they learn it.

One founder explained to me that when he was a child, he fell in love with video games. Instead of being satisfied with just playing games, though, he had an insatiable urge to learn how they worked. He wanted to learn how to write them. He didn't have access to a computer, so he checked out a book from the library and wrote out the game code by hand. He grew up to be Patrick McKenzie (or patio11), the famous developer and entrepreneur.

Another entrepreneur was born after growing weary of the hard labor and years of work in construction. Even though he was a young man, his body was beginning to break down. He was also tired of losing friends to the violence of the illegal entrepreneurial world. An IT guy at a bank told him there was a lot of money in computers. He signed up for a computer class at a community college without any idea how to turn a computer on. He's now Ruben Gamez, the founder of Bidsketch.

4) Time

One of the entrepreneurs I interviewed told me a story about his childhood. His mother died when he was in elementary school, and his father, a physician, took him with him to the hospital in the evenings and let him mess around with the hospital's computers for hours. Sometimes with a screwdriver. Always without fear of breaking things. He explored and experimented without time pressure and without an agenda. That little boy grew up to be Hiten Shah, the co-founder of KISSmetrics, Crazy Egg, and Quick Sprout (for more on Hiten's Origin Story, check out ZenFounder episode 23).

Another founder, Jason Cohen, created complex role-playing games as a kid and then wrote manuals describing how to use them. These examples demonstrate that not only do entrepreneurs have the ingenuity to pursue something, but they also have the passion to spend hours and hours of time pursuing that topic over a period of many years.

The common thread here is that each of these entrepreneurs dedicated significant amounts of time to pursuing their passion. They had time to tinker, to fiddle, to think, to outline, to plan. And, what's more, they were willing to dedicate their free hours to their pursuits.

The themes that I just outlined show the major threads that tie great entrepreneurial minds together and also lend insights into why certain entrepreneurs are successful while others fail.

ENTREPRENEUR "TYPES": STRENGTHS AND SHADOWS

Of course, every story is unique and behind every story stands a person with dreams, relationships, plans, and ideas. But since we're talking about the stories that have shaped great businesses and ideas, I want to spend a little bit of time going through some of the main "types" of stories that I see from the pasts of entrepreneurs and how those stories affected the businesses that these men and women have created.

Carl Jung was a Swiss psychiatrist and a contemporary of Freud. He wrote extensively about the "dark side" of human personality, something he called the shadow. A simple summary of the shadow is that each of us has a side—a part of us that we try to hide—that is instinctive and irrational, and prone to bias and projection. This part of us is largely unconscious and it contains the behaviors and memories we do not want to identify with—the parts of us that we judge as largely negative.

Understanding the shadow as well as the strengths of our story is important because the shadow—the angst-filled and painful, wild part of us—is also the source of creativity and passion. Our darkness can also be our strength. These experiences and pain are often the very things that make us stronger, better, more creative, and more driven. Here are some examples of common origin stories and some insights into how different types of stories shape our shadows and our strengths:

1. The Golden Child

If you have been fortunate enough to be loved well, protected, never deeply discouraged, perhaps coddled... you have a Golden Child story. This story is good in many ways! You likely have an unsinkable belief in your own ideas. You probably have no fear when it comes to pitching yourself or your business. You inherently believe that good things will come your way. You're never afraid to try. You're full of confidence and ideas. This is a great mindset for a successful entrepreneur.

But there are some downsides to this kind of story. You may not have much experience dealing with haters—with people who are skeptical. Which means a bit of criticism or a rejection can devastate you. You may not have much practice handling a door shut in your face. You may feel paralyzed by discouragement or criticism. You may not know what to do with critical feedback. You may even struggle to listen to the opinions of others when they are inconsistent with your own.

Quick tips for the Golden Child

- Remember that failure is inevitable. Do your best to inoculate your-self against a failure-related downward spiral. Routinely do things that stretch your ability and your comfort zone. Practice failure in small ways by taking low-level risks in areas where you are not innately competent (a dance class, public speaking, trivia night). Practice tolerating not being successful when the stakes are low.
- Be aware that the people you work with may not come to the team with a foundation of acceptance and affirmation. Look for ways to encourage the people that you work with—use your confidence to build up the confidence of those around you.
- When people are critical of you, realize that your tendency will be to want to convince them that they are wrong. Rather than working to change the mind of a critic, decide if there is anything of merit

in their criticism. If yes, take the criticism. If no, let it go—release it, and move on. "Haters gonna hate."

2. The Loner

If you grew up as a loner, you probably felt like you didn't quite fit into the world around you. Because of this feeling, you likely have an incredibly valuable ability to work out problems on your own, trust your own ideas, and be comfortable making decisions. You are not addicted to the praise of other people. You think for yourself and are capable of operating without much help. Your business thrives because you are able to carry a huge load on your own and manage many different angles of a problem.

Of course, there's a flip side. It is often a challenge for you to understand the thoughts of others or the fickle wave of public opinion. You may have limited innate skill or early life practice in building consensus on a team or motivating others who are built differently than you. The emotions and motivations of other people may be somewhat mysterious to you. It may make it difficult for you to understand the needs of your employees or your customers.

Chris Lema was a middle-class kid from South America in an affluent, white high school. While he made friends in school and sports, he felt alone *all* the time. His nerdery paid off and he achieved success as the web start-up world began to take off in the San Francisco area. But it took a divorce and years of heartache to force him to stare his shadow in the face. He never figured out how to be in meaningful relationships. Rather than avoiding people and withdrawing back into nerd bliss, Chris faced his shadow head on. He is now a significant member of the WordPress community and known as a master networker and connector. His greatest weakness became his greatest strength.

Quick tips for the Loner

- Work on building a professional network. It may not seem easy or necessary from where you sit right now, but few entrepreneurs are successful without a network of personal and professional connections. You can build your network via email or social media if those forms of communication are easier for you. It will take intentional effort to build a network.

- Seek feedback from trusted customers and colleagues. Let the ideas and perspectives of others be an additional data point to help you grow your business and improve your product.

3. The Pleaser

If you grew up with parents who were difficult to please—perhaps you had a father who wanted you to be just like him, or a mother who wanted to raise a star athlete, but you were a chess-playing kinda kid—then you likely spent most of your childhood trying to figure out how to please them. Or perhaps you grew up watching your own parents fail at a business or venture and feel like your own success would help salve that wound. Whatever it is, you are driven to make others happy. Because of this feeling, you probably have a good handle on how to anticipate what your customers want and figure out how to give it to them. You know how to make your employees happy. You have a good handle on how to create a business culture that keeps employees satisfied.

The bad part? You likely spend way too much of your energy trying to keep people happy without really asking what is best for your company or you or your family. Because of this, you may stay too long in a bad partnership or working arrangement, believing that if you just rework or pivot or try harder, you'll be able to make it work. You tend to over-deliver, struggling to ship out that product without building that one more feature that will really wow your customers. You are often blinded by your desire to impress, and to be appreciated, understood, or accepted.

Quick tips for the Pleaser

- Be diligent about self-reflection. Cultivate your own internal voice, separate from the perspectives of others. Keep a daily record of highs and lows so that you practice listening to your own preferences.

- Be aware of who you are attuning yourself to. Attunement is like turning the dial of the radio to a specific station. Choose your station carefully. Not all people—not all perspectives—are equally valuable, trustworthy, or important. Rather than be a "people pleaser," tune in to a carefully selected group that can be your feedback loop.

4. The Survivor

Some of us grew up in aggressive or unstable families. Perhaps you experienced the chaos of poverty—not knowing where your next meal was coming from or whether your parents would be able to pay the electric bill. Or maybe you grew up under a cloud of abuse—and your story is full of violence, sadness, and trauma. Because of this background, you have a keen sense of how to protect yourself and how to fight for what you need. You learned painful but important lessons about tenacity, grit, and outsmarting those who would do you harm. You are indefatigable. A fighter.

For example, Steli Efti, the owner of Close.io, is a survivor. There is a part of him that believes that he is an individual who stands against the world (maybe with a middle finger raised). That makes him powerful as an individual. If something needs to be done, he does it. If something needs to be created, he creates it. He's comfortable up on stage, putting himself out there.

Being a survivor as an entrepreneur gives you an ability to stare failure in the face—you're not afraid, you've survived all kinds of things already. But the trauma in your early life may limit your ability to experience a full range of emotions. You may be very rational and calculating, but struggle to experience joy, or fail to recognize when everything is going well, which may be difficult for your team and those who are close to you. Your experience of needing to fight to survive may trickle down to your business. You may come across as too aggressive or "in your face" and your customers may struggle to warm up to you or build loyalty toward you.

Quick tips for the Survivor

- Take time to record and celebrate your successes. This acknowledgment is important for you and for your team. It may also be particularly helpful for you to keep a gratitude list or journal. Let the satisfaction of how far you've come and what you've survived fuel your drive to press forward.

- Look for ways to use your strength and fighting power to help others. Consider being a mentor or reaching out to someone else who was brought up in a rough situation. Constantly look for ways to transform your painful experiences into a superpower.

I could go on and on; there are so many life stories and so many possible ways to be shaped by our experiences. One or a combination of these stories may resonate with you. The point is not that you have to have a certain kind of past in order to be a successful entrepreneur; the point is to maximize the advantages of your past and keep an eye on the shadows so that they don't catch you while you're not looking.

Here's the thing: While the innate strengths of an entrepreneur have the potential to create products and businesses that have a huge impact on the world, the shadow has the power to derail them. Those shadows lurk behind us and disrupt our productivity and well-being, and they hinder our ability to launch. They disrupt our personal lives. They destroy our relationships. They stifle our creativity.

The key to our success is not that we get rid of the shadow (if only that were possible), but instead that we know that our shadow is right there lurking behind us and we turn around and face it.

SO HOW DO I FACE THE SHADOW?

This is obviously a question that could be (and is!) an entire book in itself. And in all honesty, for many people, it takes help from a professional to really get into the nitty-gritty details of their childhood and how it affects their work. If you feel that your childhood story—and the shadow of it—is affecting the way you run your business in a negative way, I strongly recommend getting help from a professional counselor to work through some of these details and to figure out how you can use the positive aspects of your childhood to drive success.

That said, I do have a list of ideas that I believe will help many of you get started as you turn around toward that shadow and stare it in the face.

1. Let your memories be your teacher. Don't avoid them or ignore them, but learn from them.
2. Know your personal demons as well as you can. Yes, think about them. Contemplate them. Let someone else in for a look, too. And then figure out how to get past them.
3. Whenever things aren't going well, pause for a moment to consider self-fulfilling prophecy or self-sabotage. If one of those things is happening, take steps to overcome it.
4. Don't force what has never worked for you. Instead, move in the direction that you are naturally inclined and allow your innate strengths and weaknesses to guide you.
5. See your weaknesses as liabilities and plan around them.
6. Live in the moment. Yes, it's wonderful advice. Learn to ground yourself in "this moment." Practice noticing, attending to, enjoying what is happening right now.
7. Contemplate your story. Who are you and where did you come from? And how did that story shape your values and your personality?
8. Learn to connect your past to your present. There is real power in saying, "This is where I come from, and this is who I am..."

Implement these practices and thoughts into your daily routine as a way to face the shadow and begin to really inhabit your own story. We'll return to the importance of self reflection and self understanding over the remainder of the book. This chapter is about starting at the beginning- knowing where you came from and telling the truth about how it has shaped you and your business.

3

Self-Knowledge

We humans have complex, tricky minds. As a species, we are very good at self-deception and reality distortion. How do you know if you're slipping into a funk, a depressive episode, or worse? How can you tell if your irritation toward that unhappy customer is fueled by his entitlement and failure to respect boundaries or because he is the spitting image of the narcissistic roommate that slept with your girlfriend? How do you know if the fact that you hit snooze four times this morning is simply a result of all of those late nights, or if you are staring down the barrel of burnout?

Basically, your mind isn't all that honest with you. You can't always trust what it tells you.

And that makes understanding yourself pretty darn difficult.

To some extent, the fields of psychotherapy and psychiatry have developed in response to these tendencies. Mental health professionals work with people to help them better understand themselves and work through challenging or distorted patterns of seeing the world.

Thankfully, insights about your mental well-being, interpersonal reactions, and thought patterns are not limited to the therapist's office. It is possible to get better at knowing yourself.

Self-knowledge can save you a lot of pain and suffering. If you know your most common blind spots, you can plan around them. If you know the kinds of stressors that are most likely to compromise your decision-making, you'll know how to time those decisions differently. By understanding and identifying problematic tendencies in yourself, and learning to better manage your reactions to stressful situations, you'll be able to mitigate some of your blind spots and make yourself a more effective founder, friend, and family member.

How do you know where the line between mental health and mental illness stands—and more importantly, how do you know if you have crossed it?

The fields of psychiatry and psychotherapy attempt to answer this question through a big and complex book called *The Diagnostic and Statistical Manual of Mental Disorders*, known to most people in the field as "the DSM." It's a catalog of every mental illness officially recognized by the American health community. The latest version was published in 2013 and lists 297 different mental disorders a given person could potentially have.

For an entrepreneur who is trying to gauge her own relative state of sanity, it's a little too bulky to use. (Not to mention the fact that you don't want to drag out a big book about mental disorders every time you are feeling stressed. That sounds stressful!)

Every entrepreneur—every person, for that matter—should have a basic framework for reflecting on the internal forces that shape how we think and behave. I'd like to walk you through three concepts that can form the backbone of your self-reflection framework: emotional organization (chaos vs. rigidity), thought processes (fixed mindset vs. growth mindset), and basic personality traits (extroversion vs. introversion). By understanding the basics of these concepts, you will be able to self-assess where you fall on the continuum of each one.

You may think you know who you are, but often people aren't fully aware of their own natural tendencies because they haven't taken the time to get to know themselves. Learning to better understand yourself will help you use a little do-it-yourself psychology to make your life—and your business—better.

EMOTIONAL ORGANIZATION: CHAOS VS. RIGIDITY

Philippa Perry, a British psychotherapist and the author of *How to Stay Sane*, makes the case that all of the disorders outlined in the DSM can be described as fitting into the outer edges of a chaos-rigidity continuum. People dissolve into mental illness by swinging to one side and becoming either overly rigid or overly chaotic.

I think this is a brilliant and helpful description of how we humans break down. Some people become too rigid to adapt to the situation they're in. They seek control in response to stress, and when they are in uncontrollable situations, they run the risk of becoming brittle and breaking down. Others respond to stress by relinquishing control, throwing caution to the wind, and abandoning any structure in their lives. When stressed, these folks fall into chaos.

The goal for a healthy, well-adjusted life is to stay somewhere in the middle—able to be flexible when needed, but also able to stand firm when necessary. And most healthy, well-adapted adults fall right where they should be—in the middle of the spectrum. But all of us have a tendency to lean heavily toward one side when faced with a crisis or a difficult situation—we either become overly rigid or overly chaotic.

On either end of the spectrum, the pain and impairment can become extreme. On the chaotic end, you might find people suffering from significant disorganization, feeling like they are running in all directions at once, not able to filter or stay present and oriented in the current moment. In DSM terms, the outer edges of chaos might fall under bipolar disorder, borderline personality disorder, significant attention deficit, or addiction.

On the rigid end of the spectrum, you might find high anxiety and a neurotic desire to be involved in, and control all the details of, life. In diagnostic terms, extreme rigidity takes the form of obsessive-compulsive disorder, agoraphobia, generalized anxiety, or any number of disorders where a suffering person is working very, very hard to rigidly control the many shifting variables in the world.

Know Thyself: Chaos and Rigidity

The key here is to become aware of the tendency within your personality to swing toward one side so that you can recognize your natural tendency and take steps to avoid the consequences of a swing. And that takes—you guessed it—some self-knowledge and some understanding of what your brain is likely to do. Here are some ways to tell:

You might fall onto the rigid side of the spectrum if you:

- Tend to adhere to set patterns with some intensity
- Spend time and mental energy making contingency plans
- Don't like surprise or change
- Prefer to focus on one thing at a time
- Thrive on implementing systems
- Are really concerned about the future
- Have thoughts structured around *if-then* statements
- Find yourself interested in control and prediction
- Get irritated when things aren't controllable or predictable

I won't make any grand generalizations about where entrepreneurs tend to fall on this spectrum, but if you're an entrepreneur—especially one in the tech arena—then I'm guessing some of the previous tendencies may sound familiar.

Meanwhile, if you lean more toward the chaotic side of the spectrum, you might:

- Love the freedom and flexibility to work when and where you like
- Operate according to your own sense of timing
- Be an expansive or out-of-the-box thinker
- Assume that the meeting will begin when you arrive
- Enjoy having lots of different kinds of activities going on at once
- Like the thrill of a big sales pitch or the launch of a new product (but don't really love the day-to-day work between the big moments)
- Find it distasteful to implement or adhere to systems or procedures
- Feel like you're going a million miles a minute when you have a new idea
- Feel like time is grinding to a halt when it's time to follow through

Do you recognize yourself in one of these descriptions? I quickly realized that I tend to be on the chaotic side of the spectrum, while Rob's tendency is to be more rigid. This knowledge about each other has been super important for us because we respond to stress in opposite ways. I move faster, show up late, forget things, and get more expansive. He slows down, and checks and rechecks his assumptions and his systems. If we didn't have some self-awareness of these tendencies, it would be super tough for us to support each other in times of stress.

I know, these descriptions aren't necessarily flattering, but let's dig a little deeper. Look at the lists again and ask yourself, which of those tendencies represent your strengths? How do these characteristics drive you and make you a stronger leader? And on the flip size, which of your weaknesses fit those same tendencies? Getting crystal clear on how these patterns repeat themselves in your life and in your work is what will help you work around them to find some balance.

If you feel like you fall somewhere in the middle of this continuum and aren't sure which direction you lean, awesome! You are the epitome of health. Even so, ask yourself this instructive follow-up question: "How do I respond when I'm under stress?" What's the first thing that breaks when things get rough? Do you stay up at night making spreadsheets? Or do you start letting papers pile up and misplacing your keys? When the pressure's on, do you fray at the edges? Or do you start clamping down to hold onto control? If you can't answer right now, pay attention to your reaction the next time things get stressful. Evaluate your own behavior and your actions when it counts.

It's also a good idea to ask the people around you—your partner, your siblings, your mastermind group—how you change when it's crunch time. The people closest to you probably have a pretty good sense of what you do when the stress is on. Do you follow through on things well, but act too controlling? Or do you let too many things slip through the cracks?

You'll often find these same dynamics play out in relationships as well, with one person acting as the "idea person" and the other taking charge of implementation. For instance, when you travel with your partner, are you the one coming up with activities or the one figuring out what it'll take to get there?

Opposing emotional organization strategies can be frustrating, but these tendencies can actually be a benefit to business partners. In a company with two leaders, it's common for one to be more rigid and one to be more chaotic. This is a good thing, as the two often break down into distinct roles, like the disorganized creator and systematic micromanager. They can make for great partnerships, although you can also drive each other crazy if you don't understand why your partner acts the way they do.

Additionally, both personality tendencies can benefit from hiring or finding teammates that specialize in the skills they lack, and understanding where you fall on the spectrum will help you to leverage your strengths, without developing a blind spot to some of your weaknesses.

PERSONALITY: INTROVERSION VS. EXTROVERSION

Last summer, I was at an after-party for the speakers at a prominent start-up and marketing conference. At some point in the evening, the conversation turned to my work, and it was interesting to hear that the majority of these creative, successful, internet-famous entrepreneurs self-identify as introverts. They had each been up on stage in front of hundreds of people a few hours earlier and seemed completely comfortable under the bright lights.

Perhaps that doesn't seem like a very introverted thing to do.

Likely, you have probably already done some thinking about whether you are an introvert or an extrovert. Maybe you were told that you were "the ultimate extrovert" as you led your classmates through a fundraiser in the eighth grade. Or perhaps when you chose to invite one close friend to your birthday party instead of dozens of acquaintances, you were called an introvert.

It is popular to play with these labels in circles of friends and among colleagues. Sometimes folks don't have a full understanding of what exactly those labels mean. We assume that extroverts are flashy, outrageous, dynamic people who lead the crowd, while introverts are timid, shy, and hold back while secretly wishing to be at home reading a book. These descriptions are, of course, possibilities, but they are not definitions.

Let's get back to the roots of what it means to be introverted. Jung, Freud's protégé and one of the founding fathers of modern psychiatry, initially conceived of introverts and extroverts as being two poles of a continuum. As with chaos and rigidity, most of us lean toward one direction or another, oriented more toward other people or more toward our internal world. Rarely are people 100% one or the other—it's a continuum, not two separate categories.

Know Thyself: Introversion and Extroversion

These characteristics are far from one-dimensional and instead are augmented by other personality traits; Jung himself said it's impossible to be fully one or the other. We all operate fluidly in different contexts, and each of us will have exceptions that might seem to be the opposite of our "type."

The most popular way of understanding whether someone is introverted or extroverted is in reference to how a person handles social stimulation.

Consider the following questions:

- When you are in a group setting—a party, a crowd, a lively discussion—do you feel energized or exhausted?
- Do you come home from work each day desperately looking for some alone time, or desperately looking for someone to talk to?
- If you had a free afternoon to spend in any way you chose, what would you choose to do? Would you seek solitude or company?

In Jung's original theory, though, the distinction is that an introvert's inner life is what feels most significant to them. The conversations in your head are the meat of your life and your being, and internal ideas can be sufficient and sustaining without the presence of another person. To extroverts, on the other hand, thoughts don't matter as much until they're shared with someone else.

As an entrepreneur, what I most want you to take away from this section is that neither of these personality types are perfectly fixed throughout your life. They're just labels for describing your preferences with other people, and those labels and preferences may change, grow, and morph as you do.

Many extroverts, for instance, find themselves more introverted as they get older. As you accumulate more demands and responsibility in your family and your career, as you're called on more to respond to other people's needs, you might find you don't crave stimulation in the same way. The social interactions of a 40-year-old are much more taxing on your emotional reserves than the social interactions of a 20-year-old, and after a day spent balancing children, customers, and colleagues, it's perfectly normal to need time to recharge.

Similarly, as introverts develop an understanding of the superpowers that come with a flourishing inner life, and gain competence in their career, they might feel the urge to share more of those deeply held thoughts and convictions with the world. One of the interesting insights from Rob and the other speakers at that conference was how internal and introspective they felt up on stage. Rather than feel the social stimulation of all the people in the room, the stage let them focus on their thoughts and crafting their thoughts into delivering a great speech.

The introvert vs. extrovert question is, ultimately, more about understanding what you need at each stage of your life and how to manage your own personal resources well. The first step is knowing yourself, but the second—and more important—is what to do with that awareness.

THOUGHT PROCESS: FIXED MINDSET VS. GROWTH MINDSET
Think about a puppy.

Let's make it a Labrador. A 9-pound, six-week-old Lab puppy with big brown eyes and fuzzy wrinkles all over. Pretend you brought that puppy home with you today, with a big red bow around his neck, a cute little collar with tiny bones all over it.

There's probably a part of you that wants to freeze that puppy in time, to keep him exactly the way he is right now, those cute wrinkles all over his body, tiny legs slipping and sliding across the floor every time he tries to walk. But there is also a part of you that wants the puppy to grow up. To stop chewing on your shoes, to stop yipping all night long because he wants to play, to learn to pee outside instead of on your $450 rug.

Of course, you don't really have a choice; that puppy is going to gain about 75 pounds in the next six months. He will get bigger physically. The question is whether he will emotionally, psychologically, and behaviorally mature as he grows.

That part is up to you.

There are lots of possibilities. You could make the assumption that because he's a bit dopey and floppy as a puppy, he probably isn't cut out to be a well-trained dog, so you could just let him pee in your house, let him chew your shoes, let him act like the puppy he is. Perhaps out of fear that he will get hurt with his puppy-ish clumsiness, you could just keep him in a crate all the time. You could assume that because he keeps chewing on your shoes, he's just cut out to be a chewer, so you might as well just stop buying nice things.

Or there is another possibility: You understand that your sweet puppy is constantly learning, growing, and changing. Sure, he can't quite figure out how to go outside to do his business, and he really likes those shoes, but he will learn. He has the potential to be a great dog, so you invest the time in helping him grow. You show him over and over and over where he should pee, you teach him a few good tricks, and you train him on what things are good to chew (read: bones) and what things aren't (read: your $125 black dress shoes).

How you choose to see the potential for learning is the difference between having a "fixed mindset" or a "growth mindset." These terms were originally coined by Stanford University professor of psychology, Dr. Carol Dweck. This continuum is based on her decades of research on childhood development, achievement, and success. Summarizing her immense body of research pulled together in her book *Mindset*, Dweck said, "My research has shown that the way you view yourself and your potential profoundly affects the way you lead your life." The result of that research is the dichotomy between these two ways of thinking about yourself, and in my experience, it can profoundly affect the success of your business.

According to Dweck's theory, the fixed mindset assumes our character, abilities, and intelligence are fixed within us—we're either smart, or we're not. We're either ingenious, or we're not. We're either talented, or we're not. Meanwhile, the growth mindset assumes that our skills and abilities are always a work in progress, merely the high water mark for our development and education thus far.

These beliefs are generally instilled in us early in our upbringing by our parents, teachers, and in the broader educational system. Every time a child is reinforced or labeled as inherently smart, or naturally talented, it communicates the cultural idea that those qualities are something we're born with. That doesn't sound so bad in a vacuum, but you'll see shortly how that can become a problem down the road.

On the other hand, when a child is praised for the work they put into a project, or how hard they practiced to develop a skill, they receive the message that their achievement is the result of effort, not inherent ability. In Dweck's research, this appeared to convey to children that they could develop themselves, that it is exciting to try new things, and most importantly, that their abilities are in flux and within their control.

In other words, not "fixed."

An entrepreneur operating from the growth mindset thrives on challenges, and sees failures as opportunities for growth that stretch existing abilities. A growth-oriented entrepreneur has a self-esteem that is tied to effort and learning, not the outcome of any one project. Any one skill, any one success, or any one failure is a starting point for the growth that is cultivated throughout life. The more you grow, the stronger your business will be.

A fixed mindset entrepreneur believes that if she doesn't have a skill today, then she just doesn't have it. Period. This perspective doesn't consider change over time, doesn't acknowledge the value of trying, failing, and trying again. The fixed mindset entrepreneur sees only the present moment in time—not the natural (or intentional!) acquisition of skill that comes over time. This way is akin to choosing not to train the puppy. Your puppy will still change—he's not going to stop growing into an 80-pound Lab—but without your training, that 80-pound Lab will be quite a lot to handle. So believe in your puppy—and your business—enough to have a growth mindset. Be willing to try new things, to attempt new ideas, to push beyond the boundaries of what you know and can do right now.

Know Thyself: Fixed Mindset

People who are raised with the fixed mindset generally see abilities as being a case of the "haves" and the "have-nots"—we're talented, or not talented, and those are fixed aspects about us that we don't have any control over and can't change in any meaningful way. They believe we're born a certain way, and most of our experiences in life will affirm what's already fixed within us.

If you succeed in life, it's because you were born gifted. If you don't, you weren't.

The downside of this mindset is that when things don't go our way on the first try, it assumes we don't have the ability to learn or change much, or achieve a different outcome if we try again. We assume the puppy will never learn to pee outside because he had an accident. We assume our business will never become profitable because it had one unprofitable quarter.

If you're operating from a fixed mindset, you'll be tempted to avoid challenges because failure takes on bigger significance—if you fail, it means that you were never smart or talented, and that you never will be. Instead of a failure being an isolated event, it takes on a permanent implication about who you are as a person.

Another downside of the fixed mindset is that you don't attack new challenges if you don't already know how to succeed at them. You just focus on what you know, right now in this moment, and don't allow for the possibility that new opportunities might be available to you if you learn new things. Challenges that are a little outside of your current ability become something very scary, and something to be avoided.

If you don't attack challenges—especially with a start-up—you've guaranteed you won't learn, so your business's development is hindered. This fear of failure quickly becomes a vicious cycle: You fail to develop the knowledge, ability, and skills that are key to your success, particularly as a founder, because you are afraid to fail. Because you are afraid of failure, you won't risk the effort it takes to improve your abilities, or develop the lifelong approach to learning, which you need in order to succeed as an entrepreneur. Plus, this mindset creates the belief that if you *have to apply effort* to accomplish a goal, it wasn't a goal you were meant to pursue anyway. Effort has a negative implication, because it means you don't have the innate skill or talent to get the job done.

When I was in graduate school, I worked on a grant-funded research project that eventually became the core of my dissertation, and my job was to pull together questions from a bunch of different assessment tools into one questionnaire.

In the process, I made two mistakes. I double-copied one question, and I accidentally omitted another question. They were relatively minor mistakes (my colleagues didn't even catch them in their proofreading), but they invalidated a big part of the data set we got from people who replied to the questionnaire. These minor errors had turned into big mistakes.

My advisor was upset, as you might expect, but her response was over the top and straight out of the fixed mindset playbook: "You're not good at research. You're not detail-oriented enough for this." Unfortunately, as a young psychologist, I took her criticism to heart. Even though I was only a graduate student, and even though this was my first really big project, there was no conversation about growing from the mistakes, or learning to do better. Those mistakes became proof, in her mind (and my mind), that clearly I would never be a good researcher. For a long time, I believed that to be true.

The fixed mindset is a trap, and the ramifications can be huge.

The benefit of that experience was that I never made those mistakes—or similar mistakes—again. I became a much more detail-oriented researcher and proofreader, motivated by the sting of that embarrassment. By the time I completed my degree, my proofreading and focus on detail were strengths. I was offered positions in top research programs and trusted with large data sets and projects with millions of dollars in grant funding. Unfortunately, I ended up leaving research anyway. I was too anxious about making another mistake to enjoy the work.

CULTIVATING A GROWTH MINDSET AS AN ENTREPRENEUR

Your mindset is just as important for your team as it is for you. Whether you respond to mistakes made by your team with a fixed mindset or a growth mindset can make a huge difference.

Your job as a boss and a manager is to help your employees openly and ambitiously address their mistakes so the company becomes stronger as a whole. When you respond to their mistakes with a fixed mindset, like my research advisor did, you will dramatically stunt the growth of your team and your company, because they won't learn how to do things better. But if you lead with a growth mindset, you have the ability to dramatically boost the advancement of your team and your company by encouraging them to get back up and try again and do better next time.

If you use a growth mindset as you build and lead your team, you're going to retain employees longer, and attract employees that are both willing to grow *and* willing to make bold moves to expand your business.

Helping them see that mistakes are things to be learned from and fixed in the future makes the whole team better in the long run. Mistakes are expensive, both in terms of time and money, so why not take the opportunity to yield the benefit from them? Observe how you treat skills and abilities in your business. Consider how you evaluate skills in your employees and in yourself. Make sure that you're creating a culture where instead of talent, improvement, learning, and growth are praised, and where mistakes are an opportunity for optimization, not something to be ashamed of.

COUNTERBALANCING STRATEGIES

Okay, so you have asked yourself the questions.

You have done some self-psychoanalysis.

You have a good idea in which direction you tend to skew.

So what now?

After you understand the tendencies that you naturally lean toward, you can use that understanding to become a more effective person. The key is finding ways to even out your impulses as they're happening. If you're constantly feeling like you are flying all over the place, you might need a little more structure. If you're really structured, you might need to cultivate a little more flexibility and creativity. If you tend to get a fixed mindset when things become difficult, you may need to focus so that you can observe what you're learning and how you're changing during tough times. If you tend to withdraw from networking, as it makes you feel exhausted, you should probably figure out how to engage with others in a way that fits better with you.

These are called *counterbalancing strategies.*

They are basically self-help techniques to assist you with counteracting your natural tendencies and keeping your mental state flexible and in the middle of the continuum where it is healthiest. Using counterbalancing strategies is a process of taking a critical eye to your assumptions, double-checking whether you made the best decision or the most comfortable one at the time, and bringing those questions to people in your life who may have some helpful insight. Don't fall into the trap, though, of wasting a bunch of time or emotional energy questioning *everything.* Invest time in getting a clearer, more honest sense of who you are, how you tend to react under stress, and how that can influence your decisions. Then find the systems and advisors that can help you to counterbalance your relative weaknesses and get back to work.

Here are a few ideas on places to start.

Counterbalancing Strategies for People Who Lean Toward the Chaotic Side of the Spectrum

- Take special care to rein yourself in when you're under pressure. You might be really creative and full of ideas in that state, but impulse control is often a problem, too. Slow things down. Sleep on it before concretizing a big decision.

- It may be easy for you to overcommit—your varied interests and capacity for working on multiple tracks simultaneously or in rapid succession make it very easy to say yes, yes, yes without fully evaluating the timing and feasibility of delivering on all of these projects.
- Try to come up with a few strategies to avoid expressing yourself, either in person or online, when your emotions are at their peak. Be careful to prevent impulsive outbursts that might cause lasting damage to your relationships.
- Come up with little "personal rules" like, "I'm not going to tweet when I'm angry" or "I'm not going to make decisions when I'm tired" that will help ensure you have some checks in place so you don't impulsively make a mess of your life or your business.

Counterbalancing Strategies for People Who Tend to Relate to the Rigid Side of the Spectrum

- Be aware that some of your drive for organization and structure may be driven by anxiety. Practice asking yourself if a given system is based on fear rather than necessity or convenience. If anxiety seems to be the primary driver, see if you can find a way to deal with the core issue (the core anxiety) rather than prop yourself up with a system or procedure that may give you a false sense of control.
- Make an effort to build more creativity and spontaneity into your routine. (A couple of years ago, my often-rigid husband had the word "create" tattooed on his wrist as a "gentle" reminder for himself.)
- Schedule time to consciously focus on creative and "dreaming" aspects of the business on a weekly, monthly, and yearly basis. Let there be a time and place for imagination.

Counterbalancing Strategies for People Who Tend to Be Extroverts

- Your relative ease with social interactions may make it easy for you to lead social and professional conversations. However, make sure you are actively listening to other people. There may be times when you need to hold back your own contributions to create extra space for feedback from others who may be more reticent in conversations.
- If given the chance, you'll most often choose to spend time with others—it may be easy for you to neglect your own alone time. Even the most extroverted extrovert needs a certain amount of quiet, focused time to think and reflect. Make sure to reserve some alone time into your regular schedule. And protect it. Your business, as well as your soul, will thank you.
- Don't neglect your inner life. Cultivate some inwardness by journaling, seeing a therapist, or practicing prayer or meditation.

Counterbalancing Strategies for People Who Tend to Be Introverts

- If you're a solo founder who needs to make sales calls or perform in meetings or at events, you'll need to be very careful with your schedule and your emotional reserves. Protect your downtime—especially in highly social situations—so that you have time to recharge.
- Find time every day to step aside and live in your own thoughts. This alone time is a big driver of creativity and problem-solving for an introvert.
- Look for ways to navigate social situations that are consistent with your nature. Perhaps you stay for only a half hour, or perhaps you grab a few people you want to talk to and get a table for a more focused and less overwhelming conversation.

Counterbalancing Strategies for People Who Tend to Have a Fixed Mindset

- Notice when you think or talk about yourself in fixed terms—"I'm not good at public speaking." Be intentional about changing your language from a trait (which is fixed) to a state (which is linked to a particular point in time): "I don't have a lot of experience with public speaking." "Right now, public speaking is scary for me."
- Value learning and practice growth. Pick a hobby or an activity that is new to you—something that you're not proficient in and don't know much about. Make and implement a growth plan. It doesn't really matter if it is oil painting, sailing, or programming for Android. Take yourself through the process of knowing nothing to knowing something. Notice how you learn and what parts of your learning process are replicable.
- Keep a weekly record of growth and learning. Every Friday, jot down three things that you've learned during your workweek. Get crazy enthusiastic about your own capacity to grow. Look for growth in others as well. Track growth in your team and in your family.

There are no counterbalancing strategies for a growth mindset. That's just all good. Go all in on that.

KNOW THYSELF FULLY (OR MOSTLY)

Remember what I said about our brains tricking us?

It happens—mostly because we are complex, emotional, intelligent beings who are so much more than a set of dichotomies or checkmarks next to a category. No one person is ever completely rigid or wholly extroverted or solely has a fixed mindset. Instead, each person is a fluid compilation of traits, experiences, and ideas that grow and change. (To put it bluntly: I have a growth mindset about who you are and who you can become.)

Which means you will never know thyself fully. Forever. The target will change.

You will never be able to fully predict and know how you will respond to every situation. You will, however, be able to understand your natural tendencies so that you can find strategies that will help you to be effective in your thinking... and your working.

It may seem overly-simple to say that understanding your natural tendencies in these three areas can make a big difference—but it can.

4

Mind Games: Battling Haters in your Head

I recently stumbled across an ingenious research study that was exploring the question: Do entrepreneurs love their companies like they love their children? The research team used functional magnetic resonance imaging (fMRI) to look into the brains of entrepreneurs as they looked at images of their businesses as well as images of their children. No surprise for those of us in the entrepreneurial world: Brains exhibited very similar activity when entrepreneurs looked at photos of their kids and photos of their businesses. Specifically, the fMRIs showed a suppression of the areas of the brain associated with critical assessment (posterior cingulate cortex, temporoparietal junction, and dorsomedial prefrontal cortex). The authors of the study concluded that:

> "Entrepreneurs 'in love' rely on their subjective beliefs represented in 'an inside view,' which perceives the details of one's own company as unique and ignore or underweight objective information that may undermine these beliefs…. As in interpersonal relationships, the perceived need to rely on external data to validate the qualities of one's own venture is reduced."

The take-away here is that at the neurological level, entrepreneurs are somewhat compromised in their ability to think objectively about their businesses. And we know that thinking matters a lot. A passing thought can have a huge impact on your business. A failure to carefully think through data can cost an entrepreneur big time. Not to mention that thoughts are very closely connected to how we feel. Our thoughts can help pull us out of a negative emotional spiral… or plunge us straight down into one.

Cognitive approaches to psychotherapy are based on the simple idea that our thoughts can shape our feelings and behaviors. It sounds simple enough. And it is—until you consider the fact that our brains are incredibly complex and just when you think you have everything figured out, your brain goes and thinks another thought.

As recently as a few decades ago, psychologists hadn't put much emphasis on the role that our thoughts have in shaping our feelings and behaviors. Most psychologists believed that our past and environment were the sole shapers of our lives, but in the 20th century, innovative thinkers like Aaron Beck began to pioneer the idea that our *thoughts* also influence our lives. Building on Beck's work, psychological study centered around this idea for the following several decades.

This shift toward a focus on thinking is especially relevant to entrepreneurs. Why? Because entrepreneurs tend to be unusually logical and cerebral. This focus is both a good thing and a bad thing: The messages and thoughts that are in an entrepreneur's head, and the ideas they have for their businesses, can be a huge driver of success. But these same thoughts make the entrepreneur (and the business) especially vulnerable when things start to go in a bad direction.

Don't get me wrong: It's wonderful to be a rational, analytical person that can think through emotions or reason through decisions and behavior—we all strive for that. It's often why business leaders—and the businesses they own—succeed. But those same rational, analytical people can become over-reliant on their way of looking at the world and run into serious problems when their logic starts to fall apart, or when they face a situation where their thinking becomes maladaptive or not helpful.

I spend a lot of time helping entrepreneurs develop the ability to notice patterns in their thoughts that have become unhelpful. In the psychological world, we call these "cognitive distortions" or "maladaptive cognitions." (Or, if you prefer, the recovery community likes to call this "stinkin' thinkin'.")

Sometimes, for a variety of reasons, the executive functioning tools of the frontal lobe (like logic, planning, and the ability to predict and determine behavior) stop working very well. We're biased, especially about something we're as deeply connected to as our business. Our thoughts still feel logical, but they've become skewed. They tell little white lies that have the power to be our undoing.

But all is not lost: It just means another great opportunity for a do-it-yourself psychology technique. I'm going to show you the tendencies that most of us have for stinkin' thinkin' and help you to find ways to move past those and into rational, helpful, and useful thinking patterns. Then, I'm going to show you how the way you think can, indeed, influence your business, but in a *good* way.

COGNITIVE DISTORTIONS

All of us have the capacity to observe our own thoughts and to get to know how our minds work (remember Chapter 2?), and we all have the ability to notice patterns and even detect our own biases. Similarly, each of us has the capacity to identify our natural thinking patterns and to pay attention to the times when those patterns seem to relate to negative feelings or self-destructive behavior. If you Google "cognitive distortions," you'll find plenty of lists of the most common negative thought patterns that people get sucked into. The list is essentially endless, so rather than write a 5,000-page book, I'm going to introduce you to five that I see most commonly in my work with entrepreneurs.

1. Filtering

Entrepreneurs are ambitious by nature, but that ambition carries a bit of idealism with it as well. After all, why start a business if you don't see a problem in the market and think that you can do better?

Unfortunately, though, many of the entrepreneurs I know apply this same filter to their own work as well. Rob is the king of this. When the Drip team added automation rules for the first time, people went crazy. They got lots of love from their customers on Twitter and in the Facebook user group. Some customers took the time to email Rob and his team to say how much they liked the new feature. But of course, there were a few critics. A few customers complained about the interface. A few people found the automation processes complicated to use. The criticism was clearly a minority perspective—but it is what Rob heard. It kept him up at night. It almost kept him from celebrating the great accomplishment that he and the team had completed (good thing he lives with me and I could set him straight).

It's very easy to focus on the negative details of an event or a product in your business and magnify them, ignoring all the positive things about it. Entrepreneurs as a whole generally have a bad habit of dwelling on what's incomplete and needs to be done next, or efforts that have failed, without giving equal mental attention to the things that have been successful.

To put it bluntly, many people (and especially entrepreneurs) filter out the good and focus on the bad. They get so focused on fixing things that they start dwelling on things in their business that are undone or flawed and they forget to give themselves a pat on the back. They spend their time feeling frustrated or depressed, instead of feeling the pride and accomplishment that comes from a job well done.

Filtering is an unbalanced way of evaluating your work, your product, your business, and yourself. It's fine to want to continue to improve—that's part of the secret sauce that makes entrepreneurs special, but it can't come at the cost of your self-esteem. Because as I've said many times, you are the heart of your business and when you lose that hope and positive energy, then your business is destined to do the same.

2. Polarized Thinking

Similar to a fixed mindset (remember from Chapter 3?), entrepreneurs are often prone to thinking of themselves in very black-and-white, all-or-nothing ways. One day, they think of themselves as top-of-the-world, extremely successful, and the next day, they start thinking that everything they touch is bound to fail. With polarized thinking, there are no shades of gray, or room to say, "Hey, I tried. I'm learning."

Polarized thinking comes up a lot for technical entrepreneurs. They've spent their lives developing a complicated skill set—coding and whatnot—and once their product starts taking off, all of a sudden they have to figure out how to manage people and act as a CEO. Those usually aren't skills that product people pick up while they're building their first successful tech product.

I worked with one founder who contacted me because he felt that he needed help with his hiring skills. He hired a fantastic customer success person and a great lead developer. But he struggled to hire an executive assistant and had trouble finding the right contractor to work on a specific, complex database project. In one call, he told me, "I'm just not good at hiring." I cheerfully pointed out that he was batting .500 and that is a *great* batting average.

Entrepreneurs who have a great, innovative idea may find themselves suddenly tasked with new responsibilities at which they aren't quite as skilled. They start to fixate on how bad they are at those few things, instead of accepting that they have room to grow and are learning something new. My advice: Appreciate the things you already do well! There's time to learn the rest, and no one expects you to be good at everything on day one.

3. Over-generalization

Another common challenge I see with entrepreneurs is coming to a broad conclusion that is based on a *single* piece of evidence. Maybe it's because entrepreneurs like to move fast, or tend to trust their instincts, but that tendency makes it dangerously easy to blow a single setback way out of proportion.

My friend Angela had this problem. She had the opportunity to pitch her idea to a well-known venture capital firm. She was so excited and worked incredibly hard to put together a stellar presentation. She practiced and practiced, and she nailed her delivery. But the room was filled with crickets. No questions. No comments. The funders weren't interested. She spent a ton of time and energy for nothing. Her first take-away was that her business wasn't one that would successfully entice venture capital. She stopped pursuing that route for several months, until she was convinced to try again. One bad experience threatened to determine the scope and direction of her business.

There's a big difference between anecdotal data and data that's collected over time. Long-term, continuous data allows us to infer some truth from things that happen over and over again, instead of generalizing decisions based on one event, especially one that is likely an outlier.

So what do you do when something goes wrong? Don't assume a single incident means anything. If you tried something once and it didn't work, look for ways to improve and try it again. Then, focus on the data that shows up over time. If you see a pattern of, say, difficulty managing people, then it's time to work on improving that skill set.

4. Overestimating Control

I've noticed that a lot of entrepreneurs tend to overestimate their ability to control some of the forces that shape their business. They assume they have full control—and thus full responsibility—for the many things that have the power to affect the way things go.

I got a frantic phone call from a founder friend following the abrupt resignation of her director of marketing. She was shocked and disappointed that this successful team member had decided to leave. She instantly went into a spiral of self-blame. What could she have done differently? Was her company culture sour without her realizing it? It turned out that this director of marketing was following his physician wife who was going to do some specialized training overseas. For family reasons, he decided to resign and refocus. It was completely out of the CEO's control.

Because most entrepreneurs are very driven and have chosen a career path with a high level of self-determination and responsibility, they can start to blame themselves for other people's actions, trends in the market, and other challenges over which they have absolutely no control. This isn't healthy—for obvious reasons—but it's a very common thinking pattern. It's easy to fall into a habit of taking the weight of the world on your shoulders, but sometimes bad things happen that you couldn't have seen coming.

5. Thinking About the Shoulds

The last cognitive distortion that I frequently see with entrepreneurs is something psychologists like to call the "shoulds." The "shoulds" is a list of rules that a person comes up with about how the world should be, how they should act, how other people should feel about them, and in particular, how their business should perform.

Sometimes people absorb goals from other sources that might not fit what they really want to do. Do you really *want* to increase your profits tenfold this year? Do you actually need to raise $100,000 in funding or is it just the "thing to do?" Is it a good idea to move fast to get to market even if your product isn't ready? These may be the right moves for some businesses and things that many entrepreneurs *should* do, but that may not mean it's something *you* should do.

Your business might not be ready to increase profits. You may not need $100,000 in funding. Your product may not be ready for market. The market may not be ready for you. You might not have the skillset yet to deal with those situations even if you succeed at following the trend. When you find yourself thinking, "I should do this" or "I'm supposed to do that," make sure to pause and consider whether that course of action is something that you really *should* do. If it is realistic, in line with your existing abilities, and something you actually want, then yes, proceed. Otherwise, take a pause and consider other options.

As a founder, "should" is a big word that you should pay attention to every time it pops up in your brain. But instead of following the arbitrary "shoulds" of the crowd, make your decisions based on what your current capacity is and what skills and resources are available to you, what is best for your business, and what is best for you.

DE-*STINKING* YOUR THINKING

If these kinds of thoughts or thought patterns resonate with you, this is a great opportunity for some do-it-yourself psychology. Each of these conditions can lead you down a path of emotional distress or force you into making decisions based on a single piece of data or a random internalized belief that isn't relevant to your situation. The positive? It's actually pretty easy to start correcting some of these maladaptive cognitions. Basically, you can de-stink how you think with a few intentional steps:

Step 1: Observe. Start by simply paying more attention to your thoughts, particularly when you're feeling stressed, overwhelmed, or anxious. Especially pay attention when you think words like "always," "should," "have to," "must," and "never." See if you can recognize or identify one of the five thought patterns we discussed above, as well as broad statements about yourself like, "I'm not good at this" or "I'm never going to be like that."

Step 2: Start Talking to Yourself. Once you've noticed the thought pattern that is troubling you, the second step is to sit down and have a conversation with that thought. If that sounds a little "woo-woo" to you, rest assured, it's a real psychological strategy. In psychology circles, this action is known as "self-talk." (And now you have official proof that talking to yourself is *not* crazy.)

This is your opportunity to play attorney with your thoughts, and challenge yourself to examine if what you're thinking is actually true. Run your thoughts through Beck's helpful questions:

- What's the evidence for and against this thought?
- Is there an alternative way of thinking about this?
- So what if it's true? (Alternative: What's the worst that could happen?)

For example, if you're saying to yourself, "My app isn't growing as fast as I predicted, so the technology must suck," ask yourself:

- Have I been successful at marketing other things in the past?
- Am I totally new to this process?
- Can I poke some holes in the logic here?
- What's the evidence? Where's the proof to back up the thought that I'm bad at it?

Step 3: Look at Yourself From a Different Perspective. The next step is to effectively trick yourself into adopting a more compassionate perspective. Specifically, ask if you would say the things you are thinking to a friend. Would you call your friend a failure because their app isn't growing as fast as they'd like it to?

Unfortunately, entrepreneurs are notoriously hard on themselves. I meet all sorts of founders who beat themselves up for their growth rate. They often fail to take into account extenuating circumstances—the loss of a family member, or suffering through an illness, or having a new baby, or a downswing in the global economy, or a change in Google's magic algorithms. They fail to take into account the normal ebb and flow of a start-up. They fail to take into account the struggles and ups and downs that all businesses face. Most of us would consider all of that when judging someone else's progress, but we don't look at our work through that lens.

Step 3 is an invitation to extend the same kindness to ourselves that we would to our loved ones, to talk to ourselves like we would a friend—in ways that are helpful and not condemning or overly critical. You'll end up with a much more nuanced perspective about your performance.

Step 4: Externalize Your Thoughts. The next step for keeping these negative thoughts from taking over is to externalize them. Thoughts are really powerful and can echo in our minds if we don't get them out. Whether you choose to talk to a therapist, coach, partner, friend, or mastermind group, it's really important to get an external perspective on what's going on.

Take the initiative to get your thoughts out onto the table where you and a trusted helper or peer can look at them objectively, and you can get another perspective on your struggles. Opening up can feel really vulnerable—one entrepreneur I know told me that he felt "naked" when he wrote down the thoughts he was having and shared them with the group. Yet once he did it, he realized how much incredible insight his circle had for him. Even at a minimal level, it is really helpful just to get the insight that, "Hey, my thoughts are really critical right now; it's not a nice place inside my head, and I need to be careful how I think about this problem."

Step 5: Reflect Again. If negative thoughts are still bubbling up on you, go back to step 1 and observe yourself yet again. Sit down and pay attention to how you're thinking and feeling, and focus on the kinds of things that are keeping you up at night. Observing your thoughts won't fix the problem, unfortunately, but if your negative thinking patterns are plaguing you, the best place to start is at the beginning. It's okay to give those thoughts some airtime. Listen to what those thoughts are trying to tell you. Once you've found the bug in your code, so to speak, you can start making a plan for debugging it. Look to target specific patterns of thinking that seem to be underlying the trouble you're having, and use some of these techniques to make your inner life a little bit kinder, a little more comfortable, and a little bit more efficient.

STAYING MOTIVATED IN ANY FEEDBACK LOOP

Sometimes the voices we're contending with aren't from inside our head. They can be shaped by the voices we hear around us.

In high school, Rob played football. He was decent—at least decent enough to start every game. He had some great moments as a wide receiver, and yes, they even won some games. But he wasn't great. He got a few high fives after the game, but no date requests from cheerleaders and no college coaches sitting in the athletics office asking to see him.

Rob also ran track. If any of you have seen Rob, you know that he looks much more like a track runner than a football player. His tall, lean physique is textbook track star, and so, with work and training, he won races. He won the first race he ever ran, made it to the state championships in

California (one of the most competitive states in the U.S. in his event), and set a school record that still hasn't been broken almost 25 years later. I'm sure you can imagine the feedback loop that comes from being a track star. He got write-ups in the local newspaper. His name was called over and over at the awards banquet. He received lots of praise.

And I'm sure you can guess which sport he felt motivated to pursue year after year, which sport he woke up early to train for, and which sport he had a passion for.

Part of that, of course, was the fact that he was naturally good at track. And when you're good at something, you pursue it. But similarly, he had a feedback loop that motivated that pursuit, and the more positive feedback he got, the better he got, and the more he wanted to get better.

The same goes for your business. If you are getting lots of positive feedback, if customers are loving it, if it's growing, you likely will feel motivated to keep pushing forward. Your motivation is highly linked to the success of your business. And if you're not getting positive feedback, that motivation will likely wane. You'll stop feeling the urge to work harder, to work more, to create. You'll lose that oomph.

Now, it would be really great if I could just tell you right now to listen only to the positive feedback, to pay attention to those high fives and those five-star reviews, and to allow that positive feedback to motivate you to push forward and pursue more and more. But we all know that just isn't the way business works.

You are going to get negative reviews.

There will be people who don't like your product, your app, or your idea.

Being a founder is hard, and at times, it's nearly psychologically impossible to move forward. Why? Because your business means you are putting something out there that you are vulnerable to. It's something that matters—your ideas or thoughts on display in the public realm. People may love them. But people can also disregard them. Or worse, hate them.

As entrepreneurs, we open ourselves up to the possibility that what we love and want to share is something that nobody likes or cares about. We open ourselves up to criticism, negative backlash, haters, and a negative feedback loop. But we also open ourselves up to something that can be even more frightening: silence. A silent feedback loop, one where nobody seems to notice or care about your business, can be the most deafening and defeating feedback loop of all.

There will be days when your business doesn't win first prize for innovation, when your revenue curve stays flat for yet another month, when you start to wonder if things will ever swing upward. The days when you are trying to play football, but you're really built to run track, so your performance is seemingly average—those are the times when it is hardest to stay motivated.

How do you keep moving forward when your feedback loop isn't cheering you on? Here are a few thoughts I have on how you can allow feedback—yes, negative feedback—to motivate you to move forward:

1. **Ask Yourself: "Is it really as bad as I think it is?"**

   When the worst happens—you get a negative review or a scathing email—it feels heart-stopping. There have been times when I have been physically nauseous when I've received criticism, and I wanted to just give up right then and there. When you get negative feedback, the first thing you should do is ask yourself, "How bad is it?"

   For most people, there is a fear of negative feedback that causes it to feel like a worst-case scenario in their mind. But often, the fear and anticipation is much worse than the actual feedback. So, before you allow the criticism to derail you, ask yourself how bad it really is. Was it one negative review in a sea of hundreds of positive reviews? Is it something that will greatly affect your business's viability? Is it even true? These questions can help you to settle the panic and to consider how to move forward.

2. **Consider the Source**

   My friend Jessica is an author. One day, she woke up to find scathing, one-star reviews on every single one of her books, written by a woman named Jenny. On one book, Jenny said "the writing was terrible," and on another, that the "book was clearly written by an idiot who had no expertise in that area." A few minutes later, Google alerts started popping up with Jessica's name. Jenny had written a series of blog posts about Jessica's books. They were long and ranty, and full of reasons that every book written by this author should be burned.

At first, my friend was devastated to have her work so clearly and decisively criticized in such a public way. She went through the normal emotions—"I'll never write another book" to "I have to get better" to "maybe I'm not cut out for this"—but then her husband suggested she consider the source. My friend started to do some research into who Jenny was.

It turned out that Jenny had gone to high school with Jessica, and there had been a slight over a prom date (yes, a prom date) in junior year where the kid that Jenny wanted to go with had asked Jessica. And while Jessica had forgotten about the situation years ago, Jenny hadn't. When Jenny noticed that Jessica was publishing books, she exacted her revenge.

It was awful and unfair, but Jessica said that once she realized that Jenny was the source of the negative reviews, her motivation came back. No longer did she wonder if she was really a bad writer, if her books were worthless, or if she wasn't cut out for it, because she knew that the negative feedback came from something else.

Likewise, if you are getting negative feedback, consider the source. If it's from a qualified, knowledgeable leader in your business area, then yes, you should probably heed the feedback. Pay attention and allow that feedback to make your business better. But if it's your high school prom date's ex-girlfriend—or a hater who seems to be bent on hurting you—then it's probably not something you should pay any attention to.

3. **Take It as Feedback Instead of Criticism and Use It**
What if the criticism is right?

What if your business model really does have a gap that needs to be closed, or what if your revenue model is stagnant for a reason, or what if your product really does have a flaw? That criticism stings, of course, but it can also be just what you need to make your business better.

When we began the ZenFounder podcast, Rob and I set up the ZenFounder.com and SherryWalling.com websites. Rob helped me buy the domains, choose a WordPress theme, set up the process to upload the audio episodes… and I took it from there. The reality is that I just haven't cultivated my tech skills. For two and a half years, I've had two websites in my email signature that kinda suck. A few of my friends and colleagues began to comment on them. One client said that he almost didn't contact me because, based on my site, he wasn't sure that I really have the entrepreneurial chops my site claimed. I was embarrassed about it, but the negative feedback was fair. The comments finally motivated me to take myself seriously enough to invest in a great professional site. I didn't like hearing that my online presence was subpar, but I did need the kick in the pants to make a change.

Back to my husband's athletic prowess: He went on to become a track star at the University of California, Davis. He ran hurdles under the coaching of Deanne Vochatzer, the head coach of the 1996 U.S. Women's Olympic Track and Field team. He stayed motivated to run throughout college while earning two engineering degrees. The feedback loop was positive. But after two years, he stopped playing football. Was that the right thing to do? Probably. Like I said before, he wasn't built to be a football player. But who knows? With his speed and agility, he could have been a great running back.

[Rob]

Ummm… no.

[end Rob]

The point is that the criticism may have a point. Don't be afraid to listen and don't be derailed by suggestions for improvement.

KEEPING CONNECTED TO YOUR TRUE SELF

It is super difficult to have a good relationship with negative feedback. And it is super difficult to keep your mind healthy and free of sabotaging or distorted thought patterns. As an entrepreneur, you'll do battle on both fronts: the internal battles with your thoughts and the external battles with other people's thoughts. And the two battles will conspire against you. Your personal internal vulnerabilities will be triggered by the feedback around you.

As we talked about in Chapter 2, the things that shape who we become as entrepreneurs are deep-seated and often based in our early life experiences. Some of us have something to prove to a parent who we disappointed as a child. Some of us have a past failure that we're trying to erase. Some of us are working to overcome the uncomfortable sense that we are not living up to our potential. Most of us, on some level or another, are terrified of failure. We all have a few deep-level vulnerabilities that can bubble to the surface in response to thoughts in our minds or feedback from others.

The specifics don't matter. What matters is recognizing the process within you. What is driving maladaptive thoughts? How do you catch them fast so that you can recognize them and say to yourself, "I don't want to give these thoughts the power to disrupt my success"? If you work at it, you'll find it's easier to make decisions based on your true self—not on all the noise. Decisions that make the most sense to you and make you happy, with less of the hesitation and discomfort you used to feel.

Imagine a house fire. When the firefighters arrive, they care only about getting you out of the building. But then once the fire is out, you have to go in and identify the cause of the fire, figure out how to stop it from happening again, and rebuild. Similarly, when your thoughts start to spiral, de-stinking your thinking will pull you out from under the stress of your negative thought patterns. Then you have to start identifying the cause of that pattern, figuring out how to stop it from happening again, and rebuilding your brain (so to speak) so that it is able to function more effectively.

Most of us "catch fire" or go wrong when our true self gets distorted. Our true self is that most essential part of us—the part under the swirl of thoughts, the part under the voices. The core. The goal is to keep your true self and your thoughts as aligned as possible. A strong sense of our true self helps protect us from distortion, bias, and blindly acting on the fears and needs that pull us in potentially counterproductive directions.

First, if you know you're entering a period of stress, you need to be proactive about shielding yourself from making decisions based on biased or inaccurate thoughts. It can be helpful to try to write down all the different pressures you feel, and give each of the voices a name. Let them be characters in a play, arguing with each other, so that they don't feel like they're all equally you. When you get clear on which voices are your mother, your father, your fears, your insecurities, and whatever else is causing your internal conflict, it'll be a lot clearer which thoughts and feelings are truly yours.

The second thing that can help is to keep clear reminders about your true self stashed in places where you'll see them. These are the core values that define you, and the person who you want to be. We mentioned Rob's "create" tattoo in the last chapter, but you don't have to go the *Memento* route for this idea to be effective. I created a painting and embedded words that are important to our family in the painting (generosity, creativity, etc.). It has hung in the various kitchens we've inhabited for the past 10 years; I pass by it every day in my home. It's a constant reminder of my values and the things I'm trying to do in my life. I know plenty of people, though, who do the same thing with trinkets or mementos on their desk. These items help to stave off the negative thoughts by providing a constant reminder of the positives—of who we are working to become.

Third, start a journal. Even if you don't consider yourself a writer, spending time putting your true self into words can be helpful for anyone. Cultivate your particular voice and get some of your more negative feelings out on paper. Notice your discomfort and fear. Create safe spaces for those voices to have an outlet. Many of the problems people run into with these sensitive emotions is declaring them unacceptable and trying to shut down their fear or brush it under the rug without getting the help they need.

Fourth, if you find you're afraid to confront your own fear, that's a sign that you're not able to be comfortable with the muckier, more vulnerable, emotional side of yourself. That's where those protective urges step in to shield you from that stress. If you make safe spaces to process and vent your hard feelings, you're much less likely to have the urge to try to kill off that part of you. (And yeah, you may need to go see a therapist.)

Part of being an entrepreneur is that you have to take risks, you have to listen to the voices, and you have to do things in public to get experience hearing your voice in the public sphere. You have to encounter both failures and successes.

Don't get me wrong, the pressures of your work and business will still likely catch you off guard—especially when you're tired, emotional, or stressed out. But by identifying the voices—and coming up with a personalized plan to battle them—you will be able to stop them from pushing you toward self-sabotage.

And you have to keep moving forward, stay motivated, and stay committed, even when the voices you're hearing aren't saying the things you want them to say.

But if that's not enough for you, the next chapter, hopefully, will be. In Chapter 5, I'm going to spend some time talking about the common mental health issues that entrepreneurs face—things like depression, anxiety, and bipolar disorder. This is not to say that stinkin' thinkin' is the cause of these issues, but simply that if you're not paying attention to your mental health—especially in a high-impact and high-stress field like yours—then you're bound to struggle. And when you struggle, your business struggles.

The moral of the story? Pay attention to your mental health before it derails you—and takes your business down in the process.

ON GRATITUDE

It's probably a bit strange to you that I put a section on gratitude right here in a chapter where I am talking about the voices in your head. But my placement is intentional—because I have found that one of the best strategies for dealing with negative thoughts is to focus on gratitude. It's really hard to grumble when you're feeling grateful, and it's even harder to spin off into negative thinking cycles when you are thinking about all of the things you have to be grateful for.

As an undergrad, I had a professor named Robert Emmons who wrote a book called *Thanks! How Practicing Gratitude Can Make You Happier.* In his research, he found that when people deliberately cultivate gratitude, it can greatly increase their well-being and happiness. The practice of gratitude is associated with better sleep, optimism, empathy, better health, attention, and the elimination of negative self-talk. It's a practice that is really powerful for our overall well-being.

It's so easy to get into those negative feedback loops and allow the voices in our heads to focus on the things that haven't gotten done, the business that's not yet launched, the customers that haven't yet been acquired. We start to feel really helpless, nearly obsessed over the incompleteness. I want to encourage you to get into the practice of shifting that focus from the incomplete to the complete. To move from negative psychology to positive psychology.

Start by just having a mini-conversation with yourself about the things you are grateful for. For me, I'm grateful that I have a tribe of friends that are my chosen family. I'm grateful that my body is strong and that my mind is (at least mostly) healthy. I'm grateful that I've been able to pursue a job that is interesting and meaningful to me. I'm grateful that I have a reliable car that is fun to drive. I'm grateful that I no longer have to go to a Laundromat, and that my kids have warm, competent teachers, and that my son's turtle is going strong despite the fact that he regularly overfeeds her…. Once you get going, you can go for a long time. I think you'll find that merely listing the things you are grateful for in your head will force the negative feedback cycles out and give you a mental restart—one that can bring your thinking back on point and help you to move forward.

5

Coming Undone

When Greg thinks back, the main thing he remembers is shame. Shame for letting down his family, parents, and friends. Shame for being perpetually broke, shame for starting and losing job after job, shame for never quite being able to get things done, to follow through, to finish.

The cycle of crippling shame had started in college when Greg struggled to sit through an hour-long lecture or to study for tests like his classmates seemed to do with ease. He failed out of school, and ashamedly watched as friends graduated and moved on to careers. He blamed it on his own laziness, and decided that the laziness would disappear if he began to pursue something he enjoyed. He moved to the big city and began to pursue a career in web development—something he had a passion for—yet the same old struggles popped up again. He found himself skipping work, sleeping until early afternoon, struggling to keep motivated to work and to keep moving forward. This cycle continued, week after week, job after job, year after year.

After five years of battling, he was on the brink of getting fired again. He was hurting his parents, as they had to financially support him; he was hurting his friends when he said he would show up and didn't; he was hurting his employers who gave him far too many chances. And worst of all, he was so full of shame that he could hardly pull himself out of bed each day.

He finally set up an appointment with a psychologist who quickly diagnosed him with attention-deficit disorder (ADD) and bipolar disorder.

Those are daunting diagnoses for anyone, but for Greg, they came with some relief. Life quickly became better in no small part because he got the medication he needed. Likewise, with therapy, he began to recognize that his struggles with school and his career were not a moral or ethical failure, but instead the equivalent of trying to run a marathon on a broken ankle.

He finally had help.

A reason for his struggles.

A name for his diagnoses.

A tool to stop the shame.

Greg got the help he needed. He worked with a psychiatrist to find the medications he needed to balance his brain chemistry. Likewise, he spent years in therapy with a psychologist working to deal with the ramifications of his illnesses. He learned to deal with the shame, to let go of his people-pleasing mentality, and to move forward.

To continue with the running metaphor, his psychiatrist is the equivalent of a doctor who sets a broken angle and treats the fracture, while the therapist is the trainer who helps you get ready to run again once you are physically healthy enough. Both are important, essential components to the recovery process, and both are essential to finishing that marathon.

I began working with entrepreneurs and members of the tech community because of stories like Greg's. Over and over again, I heard entrepreneurs share their struggles with mental illness, with depression, shame, anxiety, and hopelessness. They talked about burnout and suicidal thoughts. They talked about broken relationships and destroyed businesses.

I couldn't stand all the stories about bright, capable people suffering like this. I began to contemplate why entrepreneurs seemed to struggle in these areas and why they seemed to struggle more than the general population. It quickly became apparent that the same values that seem to ignite the spirit of entrepreneurism in people—freedom, ingenuity, adventure, and meaning—can also create a chaos of depression, anxiety, and mental illness.

A recent Danish study found that entrepreneurs (and their significant others) were more likely than non-entrepreneurs to use medication to treat anxiety and sleep problems.

The authors looked at the medical records of 6,221 entrepreneurs and 2,381 of their spouses during the first two years of a venture. The entrepreneurs were compared with 9-to-5ers who were similar on things like age, gender, marital status, living situation, medication history, and income. It is a pretty strong study.

The researchers concluded that starting a company is *not so great* for an entrepreneur's mental health.

You're not surprised, are you?

Neither am I.

Entrepreneurs are intelligent and creative. They are ambitious risk-takers; they are often impulsive and fiery. They stay up late, compensate, are independent, and have trouble leaning on others. They push hard. These are all great qualities—essential qualities for a successful leader. But they can also lead to great struggle. Add that to the stress of starting a new business, of putting yourself and your idea out there, and being an entrepreneur can be pretty tough.

Because of this stress, I've made it my mission to let the entrepreneurial community know that mental health professionals aren't scary and that conversations about mental health can be helpful to the success of a business, as well as save lives.

Greg, the man in the story above, once told me that he now believes that for any given founder, there is no better way to boost productivity for your team or staff than by making it acceptable for employees to get their mental health checked the same way that they get their physical health checked.

That's pretty profound, and Greg has the truth to back it up. That same man who spent years mired in shame, feeling as if he had let down his entire circle of family and friends, received a standing ovation at Business of Software for his talk, "Developers and Depression." He gets it. And he understands how the right help and the right support can change everything.

Because I know mental health issues can be life-altering and business-altering for entrepreneurs, I want to spend this chapter talking through the most common mental health concerns I've seen in the entrepreneur community, and telling you how to get the help you need if you recognize any of these issues in yourself.

Before I do that, I want to encourage you: If you see yourself in some of these stories, that's okay. It's normal. In fact, it can be a good thing. Greg has said many times that if he could choose, he would take being bipolar over not. He sees big pluses and minuses: His disease is his biggest strength and his biggest weakness. With therapy, he has been able to mitigate his weaknesses and play to his strengths, and pay attention to the richness that comes from the challenges he has.

His brain chemistry helps make him who he is.

And that's what makes him great.

Similarly, if you struggle with depression, anxiety, or any of the "disorders" listed below, be encouraged. Yes, you will need help, and you will struggle. But yes, you can live a meaningful, satisfying life. And through the challenges you face, it is possible that both you and your business will be better for it.

I'm going to talk through depression, anxiety, ADD, bipolar disorder, and suicidal thoughts. Each of these is connected to formal medical diagnoses—they are considered illnesses or disorders.

I don't love the term "disorder." All of us have depressed days and all of us know what anxiety feels like. Each of these disorders represent a very normal part of human life, except they can cause significant suffering and they can also be deadly. I simultaneously want to normalize mental illness—because it is incredibly common—and wave a red flag of caution, because there is no need to suffer through these experiences by yourself.

DEPRESSION

Depression is the leading cause of disability in America.

Does that surprise you?

It did me. I always assumed that most disability was caused by back pain or heart disease or illness, but depression knocks more people out of work than any other illness. It is extremely debilitating—many depressed people report feeling like they are unable to get out of bed or function at work or home in a normal way.

Additionally, depression is extremely common. About one in four of us will experience major depression at some point in our lives. A Dr. Michael Freeman at University of California, San Francisco did a study of mental health among entrepreneurs found that entrepreneurs report a higher rate of depression than the general population. About 30% of entrepreneurs say that they've experienced depression at some point during their lives. And, if you aren't one of the many who experience depression personally, then it is almost certainly going to be a family member, employee, teammate, or friend.

Depression is a tricky illness. Sometimes it creeps in slowly. Other times, it overwhelms our bodies and our lives with the force of a tsunami determined to unravel us. Either way, it often sneaks in almost unnoticed and gets worse and worse until the person is completely debilitated.

I think the biggest misconception about depression is that many people assume it's just a feeling of sadness. Depression isn't usually sadness—it is numbness, nothingness, emptiness. Depression happens when the pleasure centers within our brains become suppressed. Depressed brains are physiologically incapable of feeling pleasure. Last month, you spent hours making Pinterest decorations for a *Game of Thrones* party, and this month, you can't be bothered to watch the latest episode. You no longer care about the things that used to bring you pleasure.

A common sign that you might be experiencing depression is a significant change in eating or sleeping patterns. Maybe you're sleeping too much or not sleeping at all. Maybe you have a fierce appetite and find yourself eating an entire carton of ice cream in one sitting, or perhaps you realize that you find food disgusting and the mere thought of food nauseates you.

Perhaps the hardest thing about depression is that your mind simply turns on you. Your thinking gets fuzzy, your mind doesn't focus, everything seems foggy. Worse still, people with depression usually have powerful feelings of worthlessness and guilt. These are sometimes accompanied by thoughts of death. They begin thinking things like, "It would be better if I weren't here."

When you're depressed, your feelings aren't rational. They aren't anchored to reality. However, these same irrational, unrealistic feelings are very, very strong. It is a terrible thing to not be able to trust your own mind, but that is what depression is—an infestation of untrustworthy thoughts.

Sometimes the cause of depression is chemical, sometimes it is environmental, and sometimes it is an immune system gone haywire. No matter the cause, a depressed person cannot function in their normal life.

ANXIETY

Do you ever feel frazzled, overwhelmed, or anxious? You are not alone.

Starting a business. Leaving a job. Pouring emotion, time, and financial resources into a project. The process can reduce the smartest, most well-planned entrepreneur into an insomniac with a racing heart, chewed-up nails, and gastrointestinal chaos (that's a fancy word for *the runs*).

It really is no surprise that numerous entrepreneurs and their spouses seek help with anxiety management during the first years of their ventures. The good news is that anxiety can be managed, and maybe even used to your advantage. (Remember when Greg said he felt like his bipolar disorder was one of his strengths? Yep, anxiety can be good for a founder, too.) A certain amount of anxiety can be motivating—it keeps us sharp, aware, and performing at our peak. It tells us when something is important. But too much anxiety can be a mess and causes all sorts of negative symptoms like impulsivity, panic attacks, sleep deprivation, and the gradual breakdown of your body. Not to mention the fact that an anxious person is generally an unpleasant person to be around.

Physiologically, anxiety is designed to keep us alive. Our bodies trigger a "red alert" survival reaction in response to a threat. Fight or flight. The heart works double time to move extra blood to the arms and legs (for punching or running). Blood is diverted away from the brain and the digestive system. Respiration becomes shallow and fast, muscles contract, senses are heightened. Sleep is delayed.

It's a fantastic process... when you are being chased by a tiger.

The problem with anxiety occurs when the tiger becomes figurative, not literal. An entrepreneur's "tiger" lurks around for days, weeks, months, years... never giving the body the chance to rest and reestablish normal functioning.

Being "tiger-ready" all the time can lead to heart disease, immune suppression, muscle tension, and chronic pain. The mental components of anxiety can cause prolonged irritability and fatigue.

Anxiety is not a state of mind to be treated lightly.

Being an entrepreneur is a formative tiger. It might not directly threaten your life, but it involves significant risk to your financial livelihood; stresses your technical, organizational, and strategic skills; and can take a significant toll on your relationships with your family and friends. Running a start-up *does* pose a risk to your well-being.

The good news is you can maintain your sanity, health, and relationships in the midst of starting a venture. You can let the natural anxiety that comes from being an entrepreneur drive you. You can survive a start-up without being overly stressed. But in order to do so, you have to calibrate your anxiety. What exactly does that mean? It means that for your own health and for the health of your business, you have to do whatever you can to calm down and let your body and mind recover between tigers.

ATTENTION-DEFICIT/HYPERACTIVITY DISORDER (ADHD)

Dr. Michael Freeman, a psychiatrist at the University of California, San Francisco, found that 29% of entrepreneurs reported a history of ADHD. This number is *quite* a bit higher than the estimated prevalence of 2.5% of American adults (according to the DSM-V).

If you take that finding a few steps further, we can conclude that ADHD may be one of the factors that leads people to become entrepreneurs. Founders are smart folks with very fast, active minds who don't easily conform to the rigidity of traditional employment. They have a tendency toward impulsivity and risk tolerance. For some, their minds have a deep capacity to absorb information on numerous trajectories at once.

I think every American has heard of ADHD, but many assume it's a disorder of childhood, one that causes young kids to struggle when focusing in school or to struggle with behavior. As a culture, we look at it as a 10-year-old boy problem—something that adults shouldn't really be concerned about.

But that assumption is wrong. Many adults—male and female—struggle with ADHD. ADHD is a set of symptoms that include struggles in inattention, hyperactivity, and impulsivity. People can have problems with attention *without* problems with hyperactivity and impulsivity, just like how people can have difficulty with hyperactivity and impulsivity *without* attention problems. Often, people with this diagnosis have difficulty with both. Everyone in the population struggles with focus at times; everyone procrastinates and everyone shows impulsive behavior. But when the symptoms of lack of focus, procrastination, and impulsive behavior interfere with the quality of life or work for a person, then an ADHD diagnosis may be appropriate.

Greg, the founder I talked about in the beginning of this chapter, struggled with inattention his entire life. He remembers sitting down to study for exams in high school and college and being unable to focus for more than a minute or two. Strangely, he also remembers himself suddenly feeling hyper-focused as the clock ticked closer to the exam. He said he would spend three weeks procrastinating, unable to focus at all, and then three hours hyper-focusing. He ended up failing out of school.

Later, as an adult, he similarly struggled to focus on projects and assignments with work. He remembers falling into a cycle of shame, where he would feel shame for not performing, so he would vow to zone in and work hard, only to find himself unable to do so. It cycled downward until he had lost multiple jobs, was living off of his parents' support, and was mired in shame.

That shame exacerbated his depression.

And the depression only made it more difficult to focus.

He began to wonder if he could ever hold down a job or succeed in school.

But here's the good news: His psychiatrist prescribed a stimulant medication and explained that he would know within 15 minutes if it would work for him. Greg remembers a distinct feeling of blinders coming off and feeling like he could focus on what was in front of him.

For many people, ADHD medication can be like a light switch. Literally overnight, focus is regained, inattentiveness is diminished, and impulsivity is controlled. Amazing, right? There are also non-medication strategies that can help with attention and other ADHD symptoms. That's why I highly encourage anyone who feels they are struggling with ADHD to seek immediate professional help, because it can be life-changing.

BIPOLAR DISORDER

Greg, who has been diagnosed with both ADHD and depression, had an easy time recognizing the signs of ADHD and a relatively easy time accepting his diagnosis. But when his psychiatrist told him that he thought he was struggling with bipolar disorder as well, Greg didn't believe it.

Or perhaps he didn't want to believe it.

It is difficult to recognize the symptoms of bipolar disorder unless you look back over a long period of time. For Greg, he remembers weeks or even months of depression. He was lethargic—he would sleep 12 to 16 hours a day. It felt impossible to get out of bed. Because of that, he called himself lazy. That cycled into despair and pessimism and shame, which in turn made it more difficult to get out of bed. He also found himself excessively worrying about things.

Then, all of a sudden and for no apparent reason, he would get a huge burst of energy. Those days, he was very excited. He would fill up journals with ideas or start coding two or three new websites and spend all night working. He knew the energy wouldn't last forever, so he capitalized on every moment in a frantic burst of work.

And then he would slide back into depression.

His life was weeks of depression, interrupted by days of enthusiasm.

As I mentioned earlier, Greg believes that his bipolar disorder is his greatest strength and his greatest weakness. The bursts of energy and creativity helped him with his work. And the hope of another burst kept him moving forward during the depression. Interestingly, likely because of the creativity and increased risk tolerance that comes with bipolar disorder, there are many entrepreneurs and founders who struggle with it.

For Greg's treatment, he began taking a mood stabilizer. Unlike with his ADHD medication, no light switch went on. But three months after he began taking it, he realized that his depression had lifted. He was getting up out of bed at a decent hour every day. He was going to work and finishing projects. The terrifying and debilitatingly low lows weren't happening anymore.

WHAT TO DO IF YOU THINK YOU ARE STRUGGLING WITH DEPRESSION, ANXIETY, ADHD, OR BIPOLAR DISORDER

1. See your physician. Check your thyroid and hormone levels. Check blood pressure and cardiac function. Have a discussion about nutrition, caffeine intake, alcohol consumption, and marijuana use. All of these things can create alterations in personal biochemistry that look very much like depression, anxiety, and other forms of mental illness. If everything checks out, consider a medication trial. I'm very pragmatic about medicine—if it helps, use it. If not, don't.
2. Find a therapist. Mental illness is complex. Sometimes it is biology, sometimes it is grief or "life." Oftentimes, it's both. Find a trained professional that can help you get to the root of what is going on. Talk through your stresses and your fears. You may be thinking about things in a problematic way. A trained professional can help you find strategies to cope more effectively with the challenge of

mental illness (not to mention the stresses of starting and running a business).

3. Be extra careful with your body. Even 20 minutes of exercise a few times a week can be a powerful intervention for mental health problems. There is solid research behind yoga as a tool to relieve symptoms of depression and anxiety.

4. Reach out. An extremely common byproduct of mental illness is isolation. You don't feel good, and you don't want to be around people, so you feel increasingly lonely and crappy. Find someone that you can sit with when you feel bad. You don't have to talk or spill your guts; simply being in the presence of another person helps. So find something fulfilling to do with a friend or family member—watch a movie, go for a walk, sit together in a coffee shop with a book in front of you. Practice asking for help. Alleviate the pressure valves wherever you can. Invite others into your thoughts so that you do not carry all of the burden alone.

5. Experience the satisfaction of solving a solvable problem. Do something each day that you know you can do and do well. Make toast, learn a line of music, walk a mile. Let your brain experience the satisfaction of completion. Done and done. Your brain loves that.

6. Keep a gratitude list. Every day, write down five things that you are grateful for. This is a simple but powerful intervention that will help alleviate the burn of what isn't finished or the worries about what isn't okay.

7. Write. Your thoughts might be distorted and loud. Get them out on paper so that you are able to look at them with a bit of objectivity. Don't let your thought patterns become who you are. Write whatever comes to your mind. Write every day for 20 minutes or write whenever your mind feels especially dark.

I talk more about these and other self-care strategies in the coming chapters, but this list is here to get you started.

SUICIDAL THOUGHTS

We've lost amazing, ingenious, and kind founders to suicide.

It's terrible. Great siblings, friends, mothers and fathers, daughters and sons, ingenious business leaders, creative thought leaders, and brilliant inventors have been lost in a way that is avoidable and tragic.

To be honest, I'm not going to spend much time on suicide because it is a book in itself—a few short paragraphs simply cannot begin to address this topic. Suicidal thoughts are common. You're not "crazy" if you have moments of feeling as if you'd like your struggles to stop. Permanently. But suicide is a permanent "solution" to a temporary problem. You are never really trapped. I promise you. Whatever you feel in your dark moments, is passing.

Many of my conversations with founders remind me of the story of Icarus. He felt delight and euphoria about his wings. He loved to fly and he wanted to soar and see how high he could go. But by flying too close to the sun his ultimate joy became his undoing. Those of us who craft our own lives, run the risk of creating unwieldy situations. Of flying higher than our wings can actually go.

If you're feeling like you're flying too high and you're scared that you'll be your own undoing. Take some time on the ground. When suicidal thoughts enter your mind, let yourself stop and wait. Go to bed. Binge watch the *West Wing*. Let time pass until the feeling shifts.

This is a reminder to be careful and watch out for each other. Watch your family, friends, and co-founders and watch for the signs that they are struggling. Be okay with talking about your dark thoughts. Be brave enough to listen to the struggles of other people.

And if you think you need help, seek help.

Poem by Dr. Jennifer Michael Hecht in her book, *Stay: A History of Suicide and the Philosophies Against It*:

Poison yourself, it poisons the well;
shoot yourself, it cracks the bio-dome.
I will give badges to everyone who's figured

this out about suicide, and hence
refused it. I am grateful. Stay. Thank
you for staying. Please stay. You
are my hero for staying. I know
about it, and am grateful you stay.
Eat a donut. Rhyme opus with lotus.
Rope is bogus, psychosis. Stay.
Hocus Pocus. Hocus Pocus.
Dare not to kill yourself. I won't either.

FINDING MEANING AND CONNECTIVITY IN ORDER TO MOVE FORWARD

This chapter was tough, wasn't it? It was tough to write, and I'm sure it was tough to read. But I also believe it is one of the most important parts of this book.

On the show *MasterChef*, they have the contestants make a "signature dish" for the judges. They call these dishes "you on a plate." The contestants have to put themselves—their culture, their passion, their likes, their dislikes, their creativity, their gifts, their struggles—on that plate and present it to the judges. If a contestant struggles with confidence, they may not have the courage to play with unique flavors or ingredients. If a contestant struggles with creativity, they may not have the ability to make a beautiful presentation. And if a contestant struggles with passion, then their plate will be boring and flavorless.

Your business is "you on a plate." Everything that you are—your culture, your passion, your likes, your dislikes, your creativity, your gifts, your struggles—is right there for the world to see. Which means if you are struggling, then your business is struggling. This is why taking care of your mental health is so essential—especially for your family and your relationships, but also for your business and health.

Entrepreneurs struggle with mental illness—specifically depression, anxiety, ADHD, bipolar disorder, and suicidal tendencies—at a higher rate than the general population. There is a reason: The highly passionate, highly engaged, highly creative personality of an entrepreneur coupled with the values of freedom, ingenuity, adventure, and meaning lends itself to mental illness. It's one of those take the good with the bad things. A highly emotional, highly passionate person is likely to struggle with depression and anxiety.

So what do you do?

The first step is being aware: Yes, entrepreneurs are likely to struggle, so be ready to recognize the signs in yourself, your friends and family, and your business partners. Seek help when you need it. Watch for the signs and symptoms. Don't be afraid to intervene.

Second, if you're feeling bad, really bad, the best thing that you can do is stop and wait. I know, that doesn't sound very profound or therapeutic. But our emotions and perspective change all the time. In the midst of depression, burnout, or suicidal thoughts, our minds can become untrustworthy. It is okay to call time-out, take a day or three away from your business, and binge-watch some Netflix. Buy yourself time. Give your mind a break from itself.

Third, it is because of an untrustworthy mind that reaching out to someone else is incredibly helpful in the midst of mental health struggles. Let someone double-check your thoughts and conclusions. A professional therapist or psychiatrist is ideal, but a friend or family member can be helpful, too. Make sure you are around someone who is easy to be with, who loves you, and who can tolerate you not being okay. They can wait with you—until your mind bounces back or until you get the treatment you need. If you don't have a person like this in your life and you're still in the process of establishing your professional resources, spend time with an animal. A dog is a perfect companion when you need an uncomplicated connection.

Fourth, when you are having a mental health crisis, return to the things that you value most. What gets you out of your own head? What gives you meaning? What causes rouse you? Seek the meaning that inspired you to create your business in the beginning. Seek the people who bring you meaning. And seek the values that make you the strong, creative entrepreneur that you are.

6

On Getting Things Done

To recap, we've been talking a whole lot about how your mental health affects who you are and how you work. We've talked about how the ideologies that got you here
—freedom, adventure, ingenuity, and meaning—may be what drove you to become an entrepreneur to begin with. Then we talked about how your childhood changed (and still changes) how you look at the world and how you approach work, projects, and relationships. We also talked a lot about what it looks like to come undone and battle the demons of mental illness, and suicidal thoughts.

We've been looking at the big picture, and now we're going to take it down a level and look at the details—the little tiny things. We'll talk about whether you should go on a 20-minute jog this morning or what to do when you're sitting at your computer at 9:00 p.m. and just don't have it in you to answer that email. We'll talk about that teeny-tiny number next to the word "inbox" and how it affects you. And yes, we'll even talk about whether you should log off at 4:30 p.m. or 8:30 p.m.

Why am I devoting an entire chapter to decisions and ideas as mundane as these? Because while they are small factors in your workday, when added together, they become the big picture. Little things, like how you structure your work schedule, order your priorities, and manage email, can quickly zap productivity in a way that no big-picture problem can, and can often leave you feeling stressed, overwhelmed, and unable to continue. In this chapter, we'll cover the why and how of setting goals, and strategies for motivating yourself to work toward those goals so that you can be productive and effective in your work.

FINDING YOUR WHY

We can't really jump into how to get things done until we really tackle *why* you're getting things done. Every idea, every business, every entrepreneur is driven by a deeper purpose and intention. If you don't have a why, you have nothing that drives you to press through difficult times, to stay motivated, and to keep moving forward.

One of my founder friends told me that she wants to be "a significant voice in the tech world." That's a huge dream—and one that is attainable for her; she's really smart and creative, and knows how to code like no one's business. This is her why. This dream is the foundation for her goals, her to-do lists, her planning retreats, her daily work life, and her entire career. I call this a meta-goal—it's not concrete or measurable, it's not something that can be attained at a certain time, but it's an overarching "why" to all of the work she will do, all of the goals she will set, and all of the decisions she will make.

For some founders, this why or meta-goal is that they want to leave a legacy in their lives—to be someone that their kids can appreciate. For others, it may be to set up a living situation that is financially stable or where there is freedom to pursue recreation or family time. For others, it may be to solve a problem that will make the lives of many people easier and more functional.

Whatever your why is, it should become the filter through which every decision in your work life is made. It is what shapes your goals, what inspires your to-do list, and what determines your daily work. It is the bottom line that guides everything else. It is foundational, but not set in concrete. Your why changes. It is shaped by your personal development, where you are in your career, and the factors that are shaping your life. A young, fresh entrepreneur may set out to identify a niche, jump in with both feet so that she can establish herself, and make a significant mark. A founder who is also a mom of young kids may be driven to create a business model that maximizes passive income and gives her freedom over her schedule so that she can flex her time around her family. A successful serial founder with 25 years of experience may be most focused on leaving a legacy. Your why can morph and change and grow with you. It can be tossed aside and revived, and it can be static or flowing.

We're never really done asking ourselves why.

So how do you figure out your why? That depends on you. I think there are two strategies that people use. The first is *outside-in*. This tends to be Rob's strategy. He spends time examining the tasks that make up his life. He considers his personal and business goals. He looks at the ways that he has elected to spend his life. From that raw material, he finds the theme—the why—that underlies the moments in his life. He's already thoughtfully chosen how to spend his time. The big-picture why is based on the small-picture, minute realities of life.

This path may seem a bit out of order—the why follows the actions. But I actually think it is the most honest, down-to-earth strategy. You are already living your life and that is the most relevant data. Look at the schedule; look at the investments of time, energy, and resources; look at all the little choices that comprise your life and ask why—and the present reality and future goals should tell a cohesive story. If they don't, changes need to be made. An aspirational why can help realign present reality and future goals so that there is no longer incongruence.

I work a little differently. My why comes from an *inside-out* strategy. I'm (sometimes painfully) introspective. I begin with the big picture. I spend a lot of time contemplating my why before I start setting goals or work plans. I journal and retreat to solitude, and really make sure I have solid meta-goals before I move forward. Then, I realign my lifestyle, daily decisions, and future goals to make sure that each goal fits to bring me closer to my why.

Right now, I'm in a phase where I have young kids at home. I'm also trying to support my dad as he battles cancer and my mom who has a serious chronic illness. My primary work, the ZenFounder consulting firm, is committed to supporting the mental health needs of entrepreneurs and their families. As of this writing, my why is much less about execution of big meta-goals and much more about connecting—being present with my family and my clients. Before, when I was just starting my career as a psychologist, my why was to learn as much as I could about my chosen field and to really dive into the human mind so that I could establish myself as an expert with a stellar academic curriculum vitae. Now I'm much more value-driven than task-driven. My why right now is to be present, to listen, to show up, to be there for the people in my life.

Whether you articulate it based from the *outside-in* or the *inside-out*, your why becomes the basis for your goals. The goals are the "what." What are you going to do with *your one wild and precious life* (to quote Mary Oliver's poem "Wild Geese")?

SETTING GOALS

Masochism is the best starting point for goals. What kind of pain are you willing to inflict on yourself? What level of suffering do you choose?

We all want things. In a perfect world, most of us want to be well-loved, attractive, intelligent, rich, influential, respected, known, athletic... and perhaps immortal. Unless you've won the genetic lottery, the effort required to maintain even one of these aspirations is significant. Goal setting begins with what pain you'll pick in exchange for what success you want. What hard thing do you want to do? When deciding what business to start, how many books to write, or which conferences to present at, every goal or decision has to be weighed against the pain or cost it will require to attain that goal.

As you're setting goals, you have to do a reality check. What are you sacrificing if you really want to achieve what you want to achieve? Are you going to sacrifice sanity, toy with burnout, hurt your family, or destroy your health to reach that goal? Entrepreneurs are ambitious, so make sure your goals not only align with your vision, but with your lifestyle.

The reality is that you can't do everything. If you want to get things done, you have to be razor sharp about where you're spending your time. Goals are the roadmap that guides the millions of decisions you make in a day about where to focus and how to spend your limited energy.

Successful entrepreneurs are master goal setters. A few years ago, Rob and I did a series of in-depth interviews about how successful entrepreneurs set goals. I can't think of a single founder that I know or I've interviewed who doesn't intentionally set goals and strategically work toward them. Surprisingly (or perhaps not surprisingly), the founders we interviewed all seem to follow the same general best practices when it comes to goal setting—even folks who work in different niches and who are in different phases of their business use the same basic practices for setting goals.

Once you set your goals, you need to monitor them and keep yourself accountable. Every founder I have talked to has a unique way of tracking their progress in reaching these goals, so once you look over the best practices, make sure to spend some time considering the best ways for you personally to monitor your goals and stay accountable to them. To start, though, let me tell you the tried-and-true, founder-tested, three-step plan for setting realistic and attainable goals that will drive your business to succeed:

Step One: Set Big Macro-Goals

Have you ever seen a flashing news report about someone who founded a world-changing start-up and their original goal had been to... learn how to use Outlook more efficiently? I didn't think so. Amazing businesses are created on a base of monumental goals—big goals that often seem out-of-reach or impossible, but that the founder believes she just might be able to pull off.

To set macro-goals, spend some time contemplating (or journaling) what your business would look like in a few years if you found yourself having the ultimate level of success. What products would you be shipping? What revenue streams would be coming in and how much money would your business be earning? How many players would be on your team?

The answers to those questions should serve as the basis for your macro-goals. Macro-goals should be long-term—most of the founders I know choose to set five-year, three-year, and annual goals. Perhaps you want to double revenue in the next three years or write a book or add six players to your team in the next 12 months. These goals should serve as the long-term vision for your company—the place that every single person is working toward and is the measure of success for a certain time period.

It's really important that your macro-goals are both difficult and attainable. For example, if you set the goal to go from earning $32,000 to earning $3.4 million during the next fiscal year, that's probably unattainable and thus will serve only to frustrate and demoralize you and your staff. Likewise, if you set the goal to earn $5 during the year, you are hardly likely to feel compelled to work hard to reach that goal. So spend the time to analyze your current business and where you want it to go, and then set macro-goals that will take a lot of work to realize but that are ultimately attainable.

While the what of having macro-goals is very consistent among successful founders—I've never interviewed a successful founder who didn't set big, overarching goals for their business—the "how" often varies. This is a place where you can figure out what works for you and how your goals can best serve you and your business. One founder I talked to goes on an annual three-day goal-setting retreat with his partners and they spend three days in a vacation rental hashing through the goals they want to set for the year. Another founder journals in solitude an hour a day for a few weeks and then writes her goals down on a vision board that hangs above her desk.

Step Two: Break Those Macro-Goals Into Smaller Micro-Goals

Imagine an author whose goal is to write a book. He writes down the macro-goal, "This year, I will write a book," and sits down in front of his computer screen and starts writing. Probably for the first few days, he will be on fire working toward that goal. He may write for hours one morning, perfecting the first few pages, and editing that introduction so it shines. But at the end of the week, when he sees eight pages out of 450 done, that motivation will probably begin to wane a bit, and by the end of week two, that blank page is likely not being touched at all.

Very few people—if any—are able to hang on to a huge macro-goal over a long period of time without small micro-goals (and thus, micro-victories) to motivate them along the way. For the author who wants to write a book, perhaps he sets a micro-goal to write a chapter every two weeks or to finish 300 words a day. These micro-goals help him to work toward the huge, 450-page goal over the course of time.

The same goes for your business. It's great that you want to double revenue this year, but if that's your macro-goal, you're not going to get very far waking up every morning saying, "I'm going to go double revenue today." So instead, set micro-goals. Maybe you want to spend month one of the fiscal year working with your creative team to brainstorm new products, or perhaps you focus the first quarter on innovative marketing techniques. Whatever they are, these clear, outlined micro-goals (or steps, if you will) will provide the scaffolding you need to reach those big macro-goals.

Step Three: Put Checkpoints in Place

Just like your big macro-goal can't be your sole motivation to work on a daily basis, the measured success of reaching your macro-goal can't be your only checkpoint to make sure you're on track. You need checkpoints to help you measure how you are progressing toward your goals.

For the author writing that book, a checkpoint could mean a weekly check-in with an editor or a writing partner to read and go over progress together. There's no way I would have finished this book without weekly check-ins with my writing partner Erin (thanks, Erin!). For the business owner doubling revenue, a checkpoint could mean a monthly meeting to analyze growth and to determine what areas are lagging. For the creator of a new product, a checkpoint could be a daily scrum meeting where progress is measured and next steps are analyzed.

The purpose of a checkpoint is to give you a measurable way to analyze your progress and make adjustments in order to ensure that you are reaching your macro-goals. These can take several forms: a daily list of tasks that you check off, a weekly report that you run, an accountability meeting with a colleague, or a weekly progress review with a master-mind group. Either way, a checkpoint ensures that you are able to adjust your progress and your micro-goals to make sure your macro-goals are met. Many founders work with, or establish, mastermind groups, or have accountability partners—I'll talk more about that later in Chapter 10. These serve as checkpoints to make sure that they have a built-in system of accountability to help them as they work through their goals.

I believe that goals help you get stuff done. With these three steps—set macro-goals, break them into micro-goals, and set checkpoints—you can and will find the capacity to work toward big goals, goals that will move your business forward. I encourage you to make goal-setting a regular and integral part of your business practices.

Once you have the why and the what, you need to focus on the how. Part of the joy of being an entrepreneur is that you get to choose the how instead of having it set for you. But you still need some strategies to help you handle these seemingly mundane aspects of your work life.

TO-DO LISTS

One of my founder friends told me that she feels like having a to-do list stifles her creativity and keeps her from being able to freely think about the problems she needs to solve. And I see her point, but I want to refute it, because while having open space to think and be creative is important, it's essential to have all of your tasks in one place. Otherwise, you risk wasting precious mental energy and time searching for your next task. Making a list—one that you use and use well—means you won't have to dwell in indecision over what to do next as you're moving on from a completed task.

There are a million ways you can structure your to-do list. I'm not going to get into how to structure to-dos here other than to say that you need to find a system that works for you; otherwise, you'll start to dread your to-do list and it will make you less productive instead of more. Trello is a great option. Rob uses Trello and Gmail in combination; if it's a quick email reply, he just writes it and is done. If it's a longer one, he sends it on to his Trello board and then it is on his to-do list for later. Some folks prefer a classic notebook and pen. Whatever it is, make sure it's a system you feel comfortable with and find easy to use. If you don't use it, it won't help you.

HOW TO PUNCH PROCRASTINATION IN THE FACE AND GET THINGS DONE

While entrepreneurs are rarely big-picture procrastinators, I often hear stories from founders about the daily struggle they have with productivity. One friend told me that he has found himself sitting in front of his computer staring at his inbox sometimes for hours, unable to pull the trigger and respond to even a single email. Others talk about a nearly crippling "fear to ship" where they have their product—whether it's something as small as a blog article or social media post or as large as a full-scale product sitting in a box ready to go to a customer—and they are simply unable to pull the trigger and send it out into the world. The product is ready, but they aren't.

Procrastination by definition is simple: Tasks—important, necessary tasks—aren't getting done. Every human struggles with procrastination from time to time. (Don't even ask me about that load of laundry that has been sitting in my dryer for three days.) But why do we procrastinate? Why do we as humans put aside tasks that must be done even though, in tandem, we are telling ourselves they really need to be done?

That answer is much more difficult to define, and that's what I'm going to spend this section talking about. But first, let me reassure you of one thing: Procrastination is not inherent laziness. It's not a lack of motivation or a lack of caring about your business. It's not some deep-seated (and therefore unchangeable) personality flaw that means you'll never be able to get things done. It's simply procrastination: a natural human reaction to tasks that feel a bit irritating or unpleasant or difficult to work on.

That alone can often help assuage the guilt and shame that come with unproductivity. Just reminding yourself that you're human and that you are responding as humans do to the task at hand helps to stop the negative self-talk and move forward. If this gentle self-acceptance isn't enough, let's go beyond that. I'll spend some time discussing the reasons behind procrastination and then give you four steps to overcome it.

SO, WHY *DO* WE PROCRASTINATE?

There are lots of big-picture—yes, there's that word again—reasons that we procrastinate. Often, it's a difficulty with priorities—we are unable to organize and reorganize our priorities in a way that helps us to get the things done that need to get done. Sometimes it's inbox paralysis—our big, filled inbox makes it difficult to know what to work on next. At times, it's stress that keeps us frozen and unable to move forward.

In order to be productive with complex tasks, you have to get into a place where your mind goes into work mode and can fully focus on the task at hand. A place where you can look at the task, dissect the task in your mind, and dig in and get it done without worrying about a wandering mind. Distraction is definitely a driver of procrastination, but ultimately, procrastination has more to do with the emotions around the task than the outward distractions that surround us.

Think about the last task that you found yourself procrastinating on. What were your feelings about the task? Were you feeling anxiety, anger, sadness, or even boredom about the task? The likelihood is that you will find that you have negative feelings about the things you tend to procrastinate on—and those negative feelings manifest themselves in an inability to get those things done.

Often, this turns into a vicious cycle of procrastination. We aren't aware of how those negative feelings affect us, so we give into them and without even realizing it, we back away from the task at hand. Then, when we don't get the task done, a sense of guilt overcomes us and we start to feel shame. Next comes the negative self-talk and we tell ourselves that we are lazy and unproductive—which, of course, causes us to have more negative feelings about the task at hand. This cycle can be difficult to break out of.

It becomes an identity and before you know it, you've started owning that you're not really productive.

And procrastination becomes who you are.

This cycle is huge among creatives—artists, musicians, designers, programmers, and inventors—and thus, entrepreneurs. When a creative sends something out into the world, there is the possibility of many negative outcomes—things like public criticism or nobody noticing or the product failing. The negative emotions that come with this fear often cause entrepreneurs to procrastinate and thus, push off the moment of reckoning when their work will be on display for all to see.

Regardless of your reasons for procrastinating, it happens. It's human nature to fail to get certain tasks done at certain times—even for the most go-get-it-done entrepreneurs out there. So give yourself a bit of kindness and allow yourself the emotional space to understand that you're not lazy or unproductive, but instead you're human. Then follow my four steps to punching that procrastination in the face.

FOUR STEPS TO GETTING YOUR WORK DONE

Now we know that procrastination is not only a very normal, very human thing that is not (can I emphasize *not*) due to some major personality or productivity flaw in you, but is also due to some very real, very normal negative emotions that are attached to certain tasks. Even with that in mind, I probably don't need to remind you that you have to get things done. Your business won't survive without it. And that means that knowing why you procrastinate isn't enough—you have to use some strategies to get up and punch it in the face so that you can get things done.

Below, I've outlined four steps to stop procrastination, but under each step, I also give you some tools you can use to accomplish that step. These tools are tactics that can be put in what I like to call your "emotion regulation tool belt"—these strategies can be used whenever you're struggling to manage the emotions that come from a certain task or part of your job. Some of these tools may work at some times and others may work at others, but just like a screwdriver, which only works to drive screws, and a hammer, which only works to drive nails, they will work only for certain situations or tasks. So it's nice to have a few options in your tool belt.

When you're struggling to punch procrastination in the face, my recommendation is to follow the four steps in order every time, but to use the tools strategically and intentionally to work your way through them. That way, you're regulating the emotions about the tasks, all while finding ways to move forward.

Step 1: Know Yourself

In order to help yourself become more productive, you have to figure out what it is that's causing you to waste time. Is it Hacker News or Twitter? Are you giving more time and attention to email than it deserves? What pulls you into an endless loop and away from productivity?

Figuring out what is causing you to waste time is figuring out what emotions are connected to the task. For example, my friend told me that she found herself procrastinating for days whenever it was time for her to publish a blog post. She would find herself writing it and then editing it, and then unable to press "post" to send it out into the world. We talked together and discovered that her issue was that she was scared of people criticizing her post—and thus, her—on social media.

Spend some time being curious about why you are procrastinating on the task at hand. Perhaps you are scared of losing money or time. Maybe you are anxious about the snowball effect of the task—if this one is successful, then more and more will come. Maybe it's lack of confidence. Fear of wasting time. Just something you don't like to do.

Whatever the emotion is, spend some time observing yourself and your reaction to it so that you can then move forward with it.

- *Procrastination Punch #1: Take Inventory*
  Look at the tasks on your to-do list and mark the ones that keep getting skipped over or are often re-prioritized. Spend some time jotting down the emotions you have when you see those tasks and considering why you feel those emotions.
- *Procrastination Punch #2: Get Into the Flow*
  There was a point in time when my husband, Rob, listened to Owl City's song "Hello Seattle" on repeat for about six hours straight for several days in a row. Why? Because the song had become a trigger for his mind to get into workflow mode, so every time he

heard it, it caused him to immediately increase productivity. Find a Pandora station or a song or two that really help your mind to focus and play them on repeat. Give yourself some context cues that let you know that it is time to get to work.

Step 2: Be Kind

A few pages ago, I explained that procrastination is often a cycle—a task brings up negative emotions, so you push it aside, which in turn causes negative self-talk, which then brings up more negative emotions. With this fact in mind, you can stop that cycle by stopping the negative self-talk, and thus allowing those negative emotions to dissipate.

When you realize that a task is causing you some trouble, rather than increase your anxiety over it, make a conscious effort to be kind to yourself about that task. Procrastination is your brain's attempt to not have to do something you don't want to do, which is an emotion-focused coping technique. Your brain is choosing to not focus on something in an attempt to feel better about the anxiety, anger, fear, or sadness that is linked to that task. So your job is to recognize this response and be kind to yourself about it.

Allow your mind to shift from emotion-focused coping to a more problem-focused approach by being compassionate with the emotions you're feeling. Spend a few minutes considering why you are feeling that way, then acknowledge what drives that behavior, and then focus on conquering the task at hand.

- *Procrastination Punch #3: Accountability*
  Find a colleague or friend who can meet with you for five minutes a day for what I call a "Stand-Up Productivity Meeting." These meetings should be fast and quick—so they don't turn into another thing that sucks productivity—and should simply be a five-minute time when you share what you did the day before, what you plan on doing today, and what stopped you from getting everything done. Just knowing that you are going to be accountable to

someone else can help you to stay productive—and help you to celebrate your successes as well.

Step 3: Visualize Your Future Self

Often, we procrastinate on tasks because we are looking at the right now. We feel negative emotions toward the task, we don't want to do it, and we are so engaged with our present self and present emotions that it's hard for us to see why we should do something that we don't feel like doing. But when you look at your tasks in the context of who you are going to be in the future, you often see exactly what you're trading up for. Sure, right now you don't want to do your accounting spreadsheet, but three weeks down the road, that spreadsheet is going to make it so you get paid.

You should never sacrifice your future self because your current self is having a three-year-old *I-don't-want-to-do-it* moment. Instead, keep the big picture in mind and realize that if an important task doesn't get done, you're only screwing yourself later. Then find a way to dig in and move on to step 4.

Step 4: Do a "D"

Now that you know the emotions behind the task, and you've been kind enough to yourself to stop the negative voice, you have to decide to do your future self proper and get on with the task. For this step, I use the "three Ds": Do it, Delegate it, or Delete it. Those are your three choices. Notice that none of those choices involves leaving it in your inbox to wallow for three days or hemming and hawing over it for a month. Just choose a D and move on.

Often, for me, the first D—just doing it—is the easiest. Just dig in, get it done, get it over with. But in some cases, delegation is best. Find the right person on your team to do the task. And finally, in some cases, the task isn't necessary. Maybe it's an email that you just don't need to answer or a job that just isn't necessary for your work. Delete it and move on.

Whichever D you choose, I also recommend that you follow the OHIO Rule: Only Handle It Once. Once you engage in a task, choose your D and finish it and move on. Don't go back and forth, don't hem and haw. Just get it done.

- *Procrastination Punch #4: Do a Power Day*
  Occasionally—and I want to emphasize that it is not humanly possible or productive to maintain this schedule for a long period of time—do a 12- to 14-hour "power day." Get away from all distractions—this could mean getting out of town or checking into a hotel or sending your kids off to a babysitter. Shut off everything, from your phone to email to Facebook. Then spend a huge chunk of time doing work and only work. While this plan is not sustainable over more than a day or two, it can be an amazing motivator if you are in a negative pattern of procrastination and low productivity. It can give you a real jump-start so that you can move forward with a normal working schedule, being much more productive.
- *Procrastination Punch #5: Do Work Sprints*
  Instead of having an eight-hour work day, break your day into smaller two- to three-hour sprints and change your location between each sprint. Maybe do three hours at home in the morning, then go into the office for another two- to three-hour sprint until lunch, then head to a coffee shop for an afternoon sprint. This schedule can help you to break your day into manageable chunks that feel much more tenable than a long work day.
- *Procrastination Punch #6: Put It as #1 on Your Agenda*
  I hate doing paperwork. I always find myself procrastinating things like forms or applications, so when I have paperwork, I schedule it as the first task on my morning agenda. That way, I get it over with at the beginning of the day and can move on to things that I enjoy more without it hovering over my head for the entire day.
- *Procrastination Punch #7: The Pomodoro Technique*
  The Pomodoro Technique—Italian for tomato—was named after an egg timer that looked like a tomato. The idea is to do a 25-minute sprint of work, and then take a five-minute break. You

set your timer, you shut out everything, and just work on the task you are procrastinating over. When the timer dings, you take a break regardless of whether you are done. Stretch, stand up, get a refill on your coffee, relax. And then reset the timer for 25 more minutes and do it again. Admittedly, it's tough to Pomodoro all day, but it's a great way to get productive on a smaller three- to four-hour task that just needs to get done. (As a side note, research shows that when you think you're focusing on a task for hours at a time, you're really not. Our brains just aren't wired to focus for that long and instead are able to focus for 10 to 40 minutes maximum. This technique allows your brain to focus for the maximum amount of time on the task at hand.)

- *Procrastination Punch #8: Timebox*
  Go through and map out your day hour by hour. Maybe 9 to 10 a.m. is for email, then 10 to 11:30 a.m. is for research, then 11:30 a.m. to 12 p.m. is for lunch. With timeboxing, nothing is left to chance, and you give yourself ample time to hammer out whatever tasks you have to do during the day.

The next time you're struggling to just push forward, give yourself the kindness (which happens to be a step in itself) to spend five minutes walking through the steps. Figure out what you're feeling, be kind about those feelings, visualize your future self, and then move forward with one of the Ds. Most of the time, these steps—in combination with a few of the tools from your tool belt—will get you over the hump and moving on to the next task on your to-do list.

ON WORK SCHEDULES AND LONG WEEKDAY BIKE RIDES

One of our founder friends, Mario, told us that he had a nasty guilt spiral over the structure of his workday. Here's what happened: Mario loves riding his road bike. He feels like the fresh air and exercise is not only good for his body, but good for his mind and soul. He believes a long bike ride clarifies his thinking and it's not uncommon for him to have an idea or two while out on the road. There are countless benefits to him going on a daily bike ride.

Yet one morning, Mario found himself wrapped in guilt as he rode. It was a weekday morning, one that he "should" have been at the office. But he didn't have anything pressing to do; his team had been notified he would be in late, and he wasn't missing meetings or causing someone else extra work. There was no reason he had to be there, but due to the whole "I must be working when the rest of the team is" mentality that is ingrained in so many workers, Mario felt guilty.

I told you in the last chapter that stress can be good for you in the right doses and at the right times—guilt can be the same. Guilt is a little voice of double-check: "Are my actions hurting anyone? Am I or is someone else going to suffer negative consequences because of my actions?" Ideally, guilt is a quick red flag in your mind that is resolved by double-checking and deciding that the risk of a negative outcome is minimal, or by deciding that the potential cost is too great and making an adjustment to your behavior.

When Mario asked himself whether his bike ride was stealing from someone else's productivity and the answer was no, that guilt needed to go away.

People often feel guilty about not doing what others may expect them to be doing or not being able to shake the feeling that they "should" be working. Many of us were brought up with a "script" that we need to work 9 to 5 or 40 hours a week. But factory hours are not ideal for most thought workers. And entrepreneurs are thought workers—most of us do our best work when we have the time and flexibility to move in and out of work tasks at our own pace. A run or a bike ride in the middle of the day is the perfect way to clear your head and optimize the productivity of your afternoon. Most thought workers, especially entrepreneurs, benefit from more customization of their work days.

It takes time to break away from the anxiety that you're behind if you're not working or that you should be working certain hours. It's not uncommon—especially if you've worked a salaried gig before and are transitioning to a new role—to feel guilt over your work hours. How do you combat the guilty feeling if it's been pushed into your mind for years?

I like the questions that Mario asked himself. Anytime you're feeling guilty, spend a few minutes asking yourself the logical "cost of this choice" questions. If they all come out clean with a firm no, then there is likely no significant issue and you should allow yourself to meet that friend for coffee, take the yoga class at noon, or hop on your road bike. It's part of the privilege of being an entrepreneur.

When I was younger, one of my teachers had a poster on his wall that had a really fancy Porsche on it, and underneath the car it said: MOTIVATION FOR HIGHER EDUCATION. I want to make a similar poster for Mario and all of the entrepreneurs like him. It would have a picture of a bike on the open road and it would say something like: MOTIVATION FOR ENTREPRENEURIALISM. That would be cool, right?

Mario wanted to break away from the "I must be working at all times" mentality, so he came to me for advice. My first advice for Mario was simple: I told him when guilt rose up about not being at work, the first step was to ask the "cost of this choice" questions:

- Am I taking someone's money? (i.e., Am I being paid to work when I'm not working?)
- Am I skipping out on a team event or meeting that I should be at?
- Is someone else going to have to pick up the load for my missed work?
- Is someone counting on me to be there?
- Am I avoiding something or procrastinating in a way that is going to cause me pain later?

If the answer to those questions is no, then you don't need to go into work. There is no reason—especially as a founder—to work a solid 9-to-5 or 8-to-6 or any other hard, long work schedule unless you are a) on a tight deadline or b) want to do so because it's how you think you are the most productive. You should never work at times when you don't need or want to just because you feel guilty. So break away from that mentality and figure out the schedule that works best for you.

Now for the hard part: What schedule works for you? I have found there are two main types of work schedules (each with hundreds of sub-schedules and possibilities that can account for everybody's personal and work-related needs). To keep it simple, we'll start with the types:

A **structured schedule** is a disciplined schedule that repeats daily and weekly at the same time, giving the entrepreneur a consistent number of hours and a consistent time to work. This is your classic 9 to 5 or 10 to 4 or 12 to 7, whether it's self-chosen or chosen for you.

A **non-structured schedule** is a more flexible, loose schedule where the entrepreneur plans to complete a given number of tasks in the week, but the time isn't set or predetermined.

In order to effectively structure your work life, you must choose one of these schedules, and then develop the dimensions of that schedule to work with your life and career goals. The dimensions must be developed based on three important factors:

- What schedule will make you most productive?
- What schedule will have the greatest positive impact on your team?
- What schedule will have the greatest positive impact on your family and personal life?

Rob works a fixed schedule—he generally works 9 to 4 every day and tries to hold to those hours firmly. That may come as a surprise to some of you who know he greatly values freedom, but he has also found that a fixed schedule works better for his job and our family at this point. He hasn't always had a fixed schedule and may not always in the future, but for now, it works for us.

The benefits of a fixed schedule are many—the main one being that when you have hours clearly set aside for work every day, you avoid the interruptions that would likely come if you weren't working. You don't end up babysitting your neighbor's kids during work, you don't have dentist appointments, or friends dropping in. Instead, your mind gets into the habit of work mode, and you are able to quickly move into a state of flow and get to work. Some people are blown away by what Rob has managed to accomplish in his "banker's hours" work day. The key is focus and protecting your time.

Interestingly, many of the people I know who have the most creative, fluid jobs stick to a very fixed schedule. For example, many writers and artists have a fixed schedule routine—they get up early, have coffee, write for a few hours, take an hour to clear their mind, write a few more hours, and then they are done for the day. It's not 9 to 5, but it is a fixed, predictable pattern. The time is protected. When they are done, they are done. No chaining themselves to the computer to get yet another chapter written at midnight and no making revisions at 4 a.m. unless they absolutely have to.

A fixed schedule is also good for a team—it helps your employees and customers to have expectations of when you (and others) will be in and available for questions or meetings so that they can be productive during their own work time. Otherwise, they may worry that they are "bothering you at home" when they call you at 9 a.m. or that they may infringe on your family time when they need you on a Saturday.

Another benefit of a fixed schedule is that it makes it easier to decide what you can say yes and no to. As a general rule, if you have a fixed work schedule, you should say no to everything non-work that is scheduled to occur during work time. A friend calls and invites you to coffee? You have to work. A neighbor gets tickets to the game? Sorry, it's during a meeting. If you have a family, this pattern makes it easier to know where you should be when, when you can help manage children's schedules, and when you just need to hire a babysitter.

Of course, there is a flip side, which is that with a non-structured schedule, you have a lot more freedom. When your schedule is free-flow and amorphous, you're able to say yes to things like appointments or coffee. This flexibility is great, and you never have to worry about missing your kid's poetry café or your best friend's luncheon. But, if you're not careful, your work time is quickly dissolved. Non-work always has the natural inclination to take over hours, so if you give yourself too much flexibility, you find yourself crunching to get work done late at night or over the weekend.

A non-standard schedule can be better for some people's personal productivity—some people just work better not having a fixed routine. They can break the day into chunks or segments—for example, spend mornings from 6 to 10 working, then take a long lazy lunch break, and then get back to it in the afternoon. Or maybe a night owl is much more productive working in the evenings than in the mornings. There is no reason to force a square peg into a round hole—or a night person into a morning-only fixed routine.

Having the flexibility to break the day into segments allows an entrepreneur to guiltlessly exercise, spend time with friends, or run errands, all while making sure they get the work done that they need. In this way, the worker spends less time worrying about a schedule and a routine and more time being focused.

Unlike Rob's work schedule, mine is unstructured. I usually have a clinic day that may be an intensive 12 hours back to back and run late into the evening. I may spend a few hours on Friday catching up with email and doing some reading. I do my thinking and writing early in the morning and usually take a nap after lunch. I have young kids who have school conferences and music lessons, and, with an unstructured schedule, I am able to plan around their schedules to make their needs fit into my work life.

I like that every day and every week is set up a bit differently. It gives a sense of freshness to my work life, which energizes me.

As an employer, offering a flexible schedule to your team is a huge benefit. While some may choose to work a standard 9 to 5, it makes employees happier and thus more productive when they have the ability to take off in the middle of the day for an appointment or to come in late and work late when they are tired. In fact, a recent study showed that most workers would choose a flexible work schedule over more pay or more benefits.

The point is, you need to choose the work schedule that works for you and your business. As a founder, you have the freedom (and you've earned it!) to choose the working hours and work flow that is best for you and your productivity. So ask yourself the questions you need to ask, figure out your own dimensions, and then move forward, guilt-free.

GETTING IT DONE

If there is a book you want to read but isn't written yet, write it.

— **Shel Silverstein**

You—my entrepreneur friends—are the writers of what hasn't been written, the dreamers of what hasn't been invented, the creators of what hasn't been created, and the doers of what has never been done.

You are the magicians behind the scenes making things happen.

You already get things done—big, important things. I hope that the strategies in this chapter serve as fuel for you to keep getting things done—to keep pressing forward, keep moving the needle, keep dreaming big, keep writing those books.

Because as Shel Silverstein also said, "All the magic I have known, I've had to make myself."

Keep making magic.

7

You Get to Be Human, Too

The founder is everything.

She is the idea person. The very beginnings of an idea were worked out at 2 a.m. in her living room, as she paced back and forth and began to wonder if maybe, yes maybe, this business just might work. She's the one who took that seed of an idea and with a whole lot of sweat, love, and tears, turned it into something. Something that works. Something life-changing.

But that was just the start of it.

Because then she kept moving forward. She came up with systems that took that idea and made it work for more people, more businesses. She solved more problems in a way that was more efficient. She found the right people to help grow that idea into something bigger than she could have imagined. She managed supply lines and human resources, coding and development, design and technical troubleshooting, accounting, and how-to-cover-the-front-desk-when-Mrs.-Jones-has-the-flu.

She is everything.

Which makes it a bit hard to believe that she is human, too.

On top of being everything for your company, you, as the founder, are also human. And with that comes all of the very real, very normal parts of being human—just like everyone else, you experience joy, exhaustion, sadness, anger, anxiety, stress, exhilaration, and ambivalence. You have times where you have to be in three places at once and your car breaks down. You make mistakes. You have days when you just don't want to get out of bed. You lose sleep, you get sick, you struggle in your relationships, you have big wins, but you also have devastating losses.

It's all part of the human experience.

And while there are likely times that you wish you could just power through in robotic efficiency, that's just not the way you were made. (Not to mention the fact that your human nature is the exact reason you are a founder to begin with. I don't see many robots running great companies.) In this chapter, I want to show you how to be human. Entrepreneurs tend to be so super-human that it can be easy to lose the human side of their life.

I'm sure you've had weeks or months when you had to convince yourself that you could push through, that if you just rolled out of bed or just stayed up two hours longer, you would solve the problems before you. You push aside the need for rest and try to manage way more than any human can. You ignore stress. You stuff away anxiety. You take a deep breath and a cough drop, and head to work when you are sick. And in doing so, you hurt your mental health, your physical health, and the health of your business.

I want to help you to manage those very human parts of who you are. To address experiences like stress, anger, and exhaustion in ways that will help you to move forward even stronger than you were before. To intentionally focus on your human side, on the emotions and experiences and frustrations—both good and bad—that come with being part of this world.

So that you can continue to be everything.

And human, too.

ACUTE STRESS VS. CHRONIC STRESS

Stress is actually a good thing.

I know it doesn't feel like it when it's 7:30 p.m. on a Friday and you have to finish a deadline before end of business on the West Coast, and there is a coding error that you just can't find. But the reality is that stress is a natural, biological response to external factors in your life. It's the quintessential fight-or-flight scenario: You come across a bear in the woods. Do you run? Or do you grab a stick and fight?

Your body is biologically prepared for both of these reactions. The instant the bear comes into view, your heart rate elevates, breathing speeds up, muscles tighten, digestion and other non-essential functions slow down or stop, and your heart begins to push blood into your extremities. Your senses become more acute, and your body becomes ready to respond.

When that bear is a huge deadline, a make-it-or-break-it presentation, or a tough decision that has to be made, that natural fight-or-flight response allows you to react in a faster, more acute way. It is not in spite of, but *because of*, your innate ability to respond to stress that you are able to meet that deadline, to nail that presentation, to make that decision.

Your stress helps you.

But notice one very important thing: You stumbled on that bear in the woods at a single point in time. The bear didn't move into your backyard and expect you to feed it. That bear is what is known in the psychological world as acute stress. Acute stress is a stressor that happens at a single point in time. It's the huge deadline that you have to make. The presentation. The board meeting. The decision. It happens, your body mechanisms step up to handle it, and you do. Then it's over.

Acute stress helps you to perform at your best, to fight problems head-on, to run faster, to focus better, to be creative and in-tune with what you need to do. Our bodies are designed for acute stress and we're very good at handling it. Our bodies know exactly what to do, and perhaps more importantly, our bodies know how to stop doing it. When the stressor goes away, your heart rate resets to normal, your muscles relax, the blood flow returns to your brain, your digestive system comes back online. And life moves forward.

Acute stress works.

There is an old research finding now integrated into psychology lore called the Yerkes-Dodson principle, which measures the relationship between stress and performance. There is a tipping point where good stress becomes too much. The body becomes overwhelmed, and performance plummets. That tipping point is different based on a variety of factors—whether the stressor is difficult to handle, whether it is novel, what emotions are involved, and how long it lasts—but the right level of stress varies. Your job as an entrepreneur (and a human) is to find that tipping point so that you don't experience what happens when you move beyond it.

When we face acute stress for a long period of time—when the bear moves into our backyard, so to speak—we begin to push our bodies to do something they weren't designed to do. This point is called chronic stress. Chronic stress can literally break down your body. It has serious and long-standing health consequences that stretch far beyond your mental health. Research has shown that nearly every chronic health problem that humans face has some relationship to chronic stress. And when I say every health problem, I mean every single one: heart disease, obesity, diabetes, irritable bowel syndrome, Crohn's disease, asthma, migraines, gastrointestinal problems, multiple sclerosis, Alzheimer's disease, cancer... and the list goes on and on.

Without getting into too much detail, the field of epigenetics is the study of how a person's environment triggers certain genes to express themselves. Researchers have found that chronic stress can trigger less-desirable genetic coding in humans, creating all sorts of serious health consequences.

Additionally, chronic stress can cause major emotional problems. People who experience chronic stress are not pleasant people. They are constantly working hard to keep it together—to keep that stress in check—and as a result, they often become impulsive, angry, and short-tempered. They make bad decisions. They may even try to cope through alcohol or substance abuse.

Sadly, in our modern culture, chronic stress has become a common element of our lives. Many of us feel chronic stress on a daily, weekly, monthly, and even yearly basis. People feel stress over their jobs and their finances, over their commute and the fact that traffic lines up for miles over the interstate, over their kids and their messy, disorganized houses. Over everything.

As a founder, this chronic stress is magnified. Not only are you experiencing all of the normal stressors that humans experience, but you also have the weight of your company on your shoulders. There is always a deadline, always a decision to be made, always a presentation or a meeting, always stressful factors. You can't escape the stress—especially when you're running a company—so instead, you have to find ways to cope with it.

I call this being a stress ninja.

Anyone who learns to be a stress ninja will be able to manage the external stressors that humans and founders face so that their bodies don't experience the negative implications of chronic stress. I'm going to spend the rest of this chapter giving you some strategies to manage chronic stress in a way that is healthy for you and your business. Basically, I'm going to teach you how to tame that bear in your backyard—he's already there, so you might as well figure out how to handle him. Because the last thing you want is for him to make his way into your house and start stealing steaks out of your refrigerator.

HOW TO BE A STRESS NINJA

A ninja is smart, stealthy, intentional, and always, always gets the job done. Often before the bear even realizes what happened. Chronic stress is one of the biggest issues that I deal with in therapy, as it is something that nearly every person on the planet deals with. Fortunately, that means there are lots of well-researched, tried, and tested techniques to deal with chronic stress. Two of the techniques that I have found to be the most effective are problem-focused coping and emotion-focused coping.

Problem-Focused Coping

A few years ago, Rob had a six-month period that was really stressful. It was right as Drip was released. Along with the typical problems of launching a start-up tech company, we were going through a time at home where parenting felt overwhelming. Rob would walk into the house after a 12-hour workday to a tornado of Legos, paper scraps, and crayons littering the floor. He felt like everywhere he turned there was a new stressor just waiting to add to his already heavy burden. The stress felt constant and all-encompassing. He woke up stressed. He had lunch while stressed. He went to bed stressed.

Around this time, Rob went on a retreat and wrote out what he called a "suck-the-life-out-of-me" list. He wrote all of the things that were causing crippling chronic stress on a sheet of paper—and then began to attack them one by one. Problem-focused coping is essentially recognizing that stress exists and then focusing on changing how to approach it. Using your ninja sword to cut out as many stressors as possible. When I work with founders using this technique, I recommend three steps:

Step 1: Take a really honest look at your stress. Write a list of your stressors from all areas of your life, including work, home, family, and relationships. Find the specific pain points.

Step 2: Problem-solve your stressors one by one. Some stressors actually are changeable or avoidable. For example, if your morning commute is causing chronic stress because you sit in 5-miles-per-hour traffic for an hour every day, then problem-solve how to fix it. Take the train or leave a half hour earlier or a half hour later. If you find yourself constantly stressed by the amount of emails sitting in your inbox, consider hiring a part-time assistant to make a first pass or respond to all non-essential emails. The point is to systematically examine each pain point and ask, "What control do I have here? How can I eliminate or decrease this experience in my life?"

Step 3: Make changes and collect data. Adjust the morning commute schedule, limit email time to two 30-minute blocks per day, and adjust your exercise routine. Implement the changes that most directly modify the sources of your stress and then track your mood—pay attention to whether or not your changes are impacting the bottom line of stress.

Problem-focused coping involves an intentional shift from passive thinking—*this stress is happening to me*—to active thinking—*I can control of some parts of my stress.* Stress is no longer a villain, and you are no longer a defenseless victim. You control how much stress you experience in your life. Problem-focused coping restores a level of calm to your body and mind, which means the long-term health effects of chronic stress are negated.

Emotion-Focused Coping

The other technique that I find really effective in dealing with chronic stress is emotion-focused coping. With this strategy, you don't attack the problem (i.e., the stressor), but instead, you attack the emotions that come with it.

It's really interesting to me as a psychologist that most cutting-edge treatments for cancer include therapy and yoga. This practice aligns with the much-researched and oft-proven fact that in order for people to heal well, they must be able to have some level of calm control over big emotions. Physiologically, humans must have controlled levels of cortisol and adrenaline in order to be healthy. Psychologically speaking, this fact means that when you can't do anything about a problem or stressor, you must change how you feel about it.

Not all stressors are "problem-solvable." For example, one of the things that Rob wrote on his "suck-the-life-out-of-him" list was that the evening routine with our kids was causing a lot of stress. That is a pretty hard problem to solve, as kids tend to be tired and cranky at the end of a long day. You can't exactly ship them off to Grandma's every night. After Rob realized the kids were stressing him out, he came up with the idea to make it a goal to create one memory every evening that the kids would have the potential to remember into adulthood. Some nights, he played a new game with them, other nights, he set up a family band in the living room and one of them played the cello and the other the guitar. Committing to doing that shifted our family's evening dynamic from one of stress—"why is the house such a mess and why is everyone so angsty"—to one of making memories. Rob said that since he knew that when he came home he would be doing something interesting and fun with the kids, the stress of "kids being kids" shifted instead to making memories with "kids being kids."

He didn't get rid of the stressor—the kids were still loud and messy and active in the evenings—but instead, he took control of the stress and approached it differently.

You can implement emotion-focused techniques in lots of ways. Rob's strategy was to *reframe the stressor* and challenge himself to take a different emotional approach. Another very simple strategy is to *counterbalance stress with calm.* This emotion-focused technique involves intentionally practicing an activity that you know will calm your emotions. This practice could mean recognizing the onset of stress and going for a run or a walk, calling a friend, sitting and reading a book, listening to a podcast, going swimming, meditating, praying, cooking a good meal and savoring the experience of eating it, or driving the long way home down the coast. The stress reaction is about going fast and speeding up in order to respond. By doing the opposite and slowing yourself down, you counteract the emotions behind the reaction and thus the stress itself.

When you employ emotion-focused coping, you're living your life in a way that allows you to cope with stress in a healthy and proactive way. One of the keys to emotion-focused coping, however, is knowing how to identify your own feelings of stress.

One thing I do in order to employ emotion-focused coping is to intentionally take time to notice physical symptoms of stress in my life. For example, I'll be in the middle of a busy day with back-to-back meetings and begin to notice that I feel a bit off. Maybe it's a headache or a tightening of my shoulders or my heart starts racing. Sometimes I just feel a bit off-kilter—defensive or anxious or quick to react in a negative way—but I've made it an intentional point to notice these reactions.

The immediate assumption is always that whatever I'm doing that moment is the stressor—but that's often not the case. So, when I feel the physical response to stress, I go backward and consider the tasks I've done throughout the day. Often, I'm responding to something much older than the immediate task at hand, and often it's a combination of stressors leading up to the stress response.

Once I've identified the stressor—or stressors—I am able to employ emotion-focused coping to handle it. Sometimes it's as simple as having a little talk with myself. Perhaps it wasn't a rational stressor. Maybe I handled the actual stressor, but my physiological response hadn't yet caught up with that fact. Maybe it's a future worry or a past concern. But whatever it is, I have a little talk with myself to figure out if my emotions and my response are in line with the reality.

Then I employ emotion-focused coping. I spend five minutes doing a few yoga exercises. I grab a cup of tea. I do whatever I need to do to stop the stress response and nurture my body back to calm. And this action allows me to attack my day—and the problems I need to solve—with a clear mind and a healthy outlook.

GO TO YOUR HAPPY PLACE

I think we've all been told once or twice to close our eyes and let our minds go to our happy place. And this advice is good (see: emotion-focused coping), but it's also possible to go beyond that mysterious happy place in your head and, instead, seek out a real, live, you-can-touch-it happy place.

In order to cope with chronic stress, you may want to have a place to go that will allow your body and mind to fully refresh. You must invest your time, your money, and your energy into experiences that are good for your emotional health—experiences that will help to reshape your perspective on your life, your work, your business, and your ideas.

For Rob and I, that is the central coast of California. We both feel peace and calm when we are by the ocean—when we are outdoors, enjoying nature, enjoying each other. So we invested our time and resources into an apartment on the coast—our "happy place." It is our way to escape and spend time together in a place that is important to us. It's where we get away as a family, where we go individually to recharge, and where we hope our boys will be able to retreat to as they learn to manage their own stressors.

For me personally, our beach apartment is my favorite way to escape the stress of my life. To be able to come regularly to a place that I love so much and can enjoy along with my kids really helps me to find emotional calm, and to recharge for my daily life. I love to watch my kids enjoy exploring and getting comfortable with the water, spending hours and hours in tide pools, and discovering different creatures and sea life. From the time he was four or five years old, my youngest son could find an octopus in a tide pool with pretty good reliability, and my kids have learned to notice, observe, and work with the ocean.

The world opens up when we are there.

Why am I telling you this? Because that's my happy place. That's my built-in place where I do my emotion-focused coping. Just thinking and writing about it right now relieves my feelings of stress—as it should. I think that every founder—every human, for that matter—should have and utilize a happy place.

Rob once told me that when he picks up his laptop, he immediately starts thinking about work and what tasks he needs to accomplish. Likewise, when he picks up his iPad—which he uses for podcasts and games with the kids—he immediately begins to relax and focus on play. Your happy place should be just that. When you get there, you should immediately start to feel relaxed—the stress slipping away, your emotions settling.

I do want to point out that we saved and planned for our beach apartment for years before it became a reality. It isn't fancy—kind of like a college kid's apartment with old carpet and mini-blinds. It doesn't really matter. It has been worth every penny, but I also recognize that not everyone is in a place to be able to purchase a happy place in the form of a beach house or mountain cabin or whatnot. That's okay! There are lots of ways to get your happy place without spending big bucks. Here are a few ideas:

- A favorite park or lake or river near your house
- A coffee shop that serves the best caramel latte ever that you can sip from a comfy chair

- A corner of your house where you have a "rest nook"—there's a comfy chair, soft lighting, a nice fluffy blanket, a beautiful photo or piece of art—and can retreat to when you want to read or listen to podcasts
- A mountain trail or overlook
- A favorite hotel or AirBNB that's close to your hometown where you can escape to
- A friend's house
- A shed or an RV that you park in your yard and fix up to be a retreat spot
- A garden

The point is, make sure you always have a place where you can reset—a physical place that your body associates with rest and calm. This place is where your mind goes into rest mode, where your mind shifts, where you are able to employ those emotion-based coping techniques and restore yourself to good health. A place where you can integrate joy and play and rest into your life, and be stronger because of it.

TAKE A VACATION

My hope is that you'd be able to visit your happy place at least twice a month.

You also need to take a vacation.

I'm making you do all sorts of crazy fun things in this chapter, aren't I? Vacation is serious business—I would argue that vacation is just as important as board meetings, conferences, and all of those other things you do to keep your business running well.

Remember all that stuff about chronic stress? Well, taking a vacation from your everyday life (and thus stress) is the best way to give yourself a reboot from all of the stress, while also giving you a better outlook on life and the motivation to achieve more. The dividends often pay off right away: Sure, you took a week or two off, but when you come back inspired and refreshed, you're likely to be more productive than you ever were before.

Nearly every founder I talk to balks at this idea.

And I get it. I own a business, as does my husband, and I understand how anxious it makes a founder feel to step away. It's hard to disconnect, especially because you are an essential (and irreplaceable) part of your business. You are the one you count on to communicate with customers, solve problems, and manage expectations. I know that for me, the idea of leaving and disconnecting from everything often feels more stressful than the idea of staying home and just keeping on.

But as a psychologist, I know to reject that thought—not because it's not valid, but instead, because you need to go on vacation anyway. Research has shown again and again that people who give their minds and bodies a break from the grind are better able to think creatively, to solve problems, to step away from the robotic just-get-it-done mindset that often comes with months and months of stress. When you step back and go on vacation, you re-energize and often come back raring to go and stoked about the things you thought of while your mind was on a break.

I like to equate life as a founder with the idea of running a marathon at sprint speed. You may start off running strong and even be able to sprint that first half-mile, but eventually it's going to catch up with you. No one is capable of running the whole 26 miles at full pelt, so if you want to sprint the whole thing, you have to build in little mini-breaks for yourself. Maybe there's a water stop at the mile marker where you grab a quick rest. And at a mile and a quarter, you grab a PowerBar. And at the 10-mile mark, you head off to Fiji to lay on the beach for a few days.

I want to give you permission—no, a prescription—to go on vacation. If the idea of completely disconnecting makes you all-out panic attack anxious, don't completely disconnect. Bring your phone along and check email a few times a day or call in for scrum meetings. Make it work for you and your personal situation. But make sure you make it work. Go. Get away. Find the time. It will pay off for you in the long run. Doctor's orders.

GOING ON A RETREAT

Going on a vacation is for your personal life. A retreat is for your business.

A vacation is a time-out, away from work. A retreat is a time-in, a deep-dive into your business.

I believe that every entrepreneur, every founder, every business leader, needs to take at least three days and go on a personal retreat each year. The more you know yourself, the better you are going to be on this journey (remember, your business *is* you) and spending time to reflect, refocus, and consider the big picture can breathe new life into both your business and your life. Additionally, it's easy to find yourself on a path that perhaps someone else told you to go down, or one that seemed right a year ago, but is no longer correct, or represents a drift away from your goals, or even one that is right, but needs some tweaking. A reflective retreat can help you to double-check your path, and find your way and your voice so that you can refocus your business to be even better.

A retreat can mean a lot of things for different people, depending on what will truly give you the solitude, space, and time to think, to reflect, and to grow. For me, I find a hotel room with a view of the ocean and pack a roll of butcher paper and a box of markers. One of my founder friends goes to her family's cabin in the woods and then retreats even further into nature on hikes so that she can really find a quiet place to think and jot things down. Another friend checks herself into a fancy hotel, orders room service, and spends the time curled up in a big feather bed, surrounded by journals and sketchbooks.

Now, I know that the mere thought of taking a few days off to do nothing but think and reflect sounds terrifying to many of you. You're already considering the logistical nightmare of stopping work for a few days, of finding someone to cover a storefront or to lead a team, of canceling meetings or rescheduling events. And I get it: Life at a business can be daunting and fast-paced. It may feel like you can't afford to take the time for a retreat, but I will flip that on its back and say you can't afford not to.

A retreat gives you time to reflect back and consider the functioning of both your business and your life. Here are some sample reflection questions:

1. What gave me life in the last year?
2. What sucked life out of me?
3. What things drove growth for my business in the last year?
4. In what situations was I most irritable, impatient, or angry?
5. When did I make an unwise decision or really lose my cool? What contributed to those experiences?
6. What do I regret? What am I embarrassed of?
7. What am I most proud of when I reflect on the past year?

Retreats are also a time to check in and really assess how you are in the present. Are you where you want to be? Consider questions like these:

8. What entrepreneurial value—freedom, ingenuity, adventure, or meaning—do I feel most drawn to at this time in my life? What can I do to pursue that value?
9. What entrepreneurial value am I not getting enough of? How can I change that?
10. Am I feeling burnt-out? Why? How can I change that?
11. What sets me apart from my peers?
12. Who do I most admire? What about them do I admire?
13. Am I using my time wisely?
14. What activities are most important to me?
15. What am I unwilling to live without?
16. How is my life different than I thought it would be at this phase of my life?
    And finally, retreats are a time to look to the future—to establish priorities and set goals.
17. In a perfect world, what new products or features would I add to my business or product to make it better?
18. Where do I see my business one year from today revenue-wise? Size-wise? Staff-wise?
19. If I had unlimited resources, what would I do next with my business?
20. How can I grow in the next year?

21. How can I shrink in the next year? (Yes, sometimes "shrinking" or cutting back is an essential component to growth as well.)
22. How can the positive events or experiences of the past year be a greater part of my life in the year ahead?
23. How can I spend more time and energy doing the most important, most meaningful activities?
24. How can I maximize my strengths in the coming year?
25. What are the most important investments I need to make over the next year?

During your retreat, spend time carefully considering the questions that are most important. You certainly won't be able to give meaningful time to all the prompts that I've listed. Write down (or record) your answers so you can go back to them over the course of your next year. Then, spend some time finding a game plan that will help you to move your business to the place you want it to be in the next year.

When I look back on my personal retreats over the years, I see them as catalysts for the times that my career and my values really changed and grew. I see those days away as times when I got to know myself, my plans, my path, and my dreams better than before, and when I found concrete ways to move forward in order to bring my business to fruition.

RETREATS AS DATA FOR BIG DECISIONS

As I've mentioned earlier in this book, I trained to be an academic psychologist and spent several years as a tenure-track professor at a teaching university. Two years in a row, I saw the same lows show up in my retreat reflections: faculty meetings, grading, high email volume about unimportant issues, boring administrative responsibilities. I couldn't ignore the fact that I was really unhappy at my teaching job. The retreats were two data points. Even though I'd spent years preparing to be a professor, my retreats helped me to clearly see that the job wasn't fitting for me. Too many of my lows were non-negotiable parts of the job. During my retreat, I made the decision to resign. It was a tremendously difficult decision because at the time, it felt like a giant U-turn in my career. But it was absolutely the right move for me.

I hate to think about how much time I would have wasted being in the wrong job had I not had a regular time and place to ask big questions about my work and life.

If the retreat idea resonates with you and you'd like more resources, we put together the ZenFounder Guide to Founder Retreats.

FIGHTING STRESS SO THAT IT FIGHTS FOR YOU

Being an entrepreneur is stressful.

Your entire business—your livelihood, your dreams, your ideas, your creativity, the dreams of others—rests on your shoulders. It's a huge undertaking, a huge task, and a huge accomplishment—one that we've already established you are well-suited for. You are everything for your company and everything depends on you.

I know that those words alone may cause you stress.

It's heavy to think of how much you are responsible for.

But it's also clarifying: Because if you are everything to your company, then your health is of utmost importance. Which means your first priority has to be taking care of your company's greatest resource: you.

So consider your stress.

Employ problem-focused and emotion-focused coping.

Go on vacation.

Find your happy place.

Intentionally find a place where you can renew and refresh.

Go on retreats.

And take care of the human that matters most to your business.

8

Mastering Disruption

In February 2017, a series of events collided to create a major disruption to my life as I knew it. My dad was diagnosed with esophageal cancer—a relatively rare cancer with a low survival rate. My parents decided to leave rural California to come to Minneapolis (where we live) so that my dad could receive a thorough evaluation and treatment plan from the world-renowned Mayo Clinic. Just as my dad was in the thick of his many, many appointments, my 30-year-old brother ended up in the intensive care unit (ICU) in Montana. Multiple organ systems were failing due to years of alcohol abuse. I'll never forget the ICU doctor saying the words, "This is really an hour-by-hour situation."

My parents were (obviously) unable to go be with my brother, so I took three trips to Montana in a three-week period. For the month of February, I spent hours and hours in hospital waiting rooms, sitting next to hospital beds, asking medical questions, and working to care for my family.

I felt like I was handling it fairly well. And then, as if to add insult to injury, I sat down in a hurried state one morning and took a huge gulp of too-hot coffee and burned my mouth. Badly, it turns out, as a few days later, I realized the pain was getting worse instead of better. A doctor's visit revealed that the burn had gotten infected, which resulted in rounds and rounds of antibiotics and ultimately, an emergency root canal.

This is the power of stress. When we have really big stressors, our body goes into high-alert. Our bodies and brains are so focused on the stressors that we get distracted (and do distracted things, like taking a huge gulp of hot coffee). We become unable to work or function normally. Additionally, due to the high stress, my immune system, which would normally be capable of fighting off a minor infection, wasn't functioning well and a little abrasion turned into a really big deal.

On top of the burn and the root canal, another symptom of my stress was parking tickets. I had never in my entire life gotten a parking ticket. But in the four weeks when I was dealing with the hospital stays and the root canals, I got four. Four! Four times, I was so distracted when I parked my car that I simply forgot to put money in the meter or read the posted signs. Four times.

Here's the thing: I consider myself a fairly calm and controlled person. I have worked hard to keep myself healthy enough so that I am up to the task of handling challenges. I have a great support system in place—family and friends—who stand by me in times of need. I am one of those people who should, by all technical standards, be able to hold it together even under high levels of stress. Yet, in spite of all of that, when huge stressors happened, the edges started to fray.

Things quickly unraveled.

The good news is that through some intentional steps, I was able to rein things back in. Rob stepped up and held down the fort, taking care of the kids and the house. I took control of my schedule and gave myself space to rest and recover. Notably, my job also helped to diffuse my stress. I kept working on a small scale during this crazy month. I enjoy my work, and working with my clients served as a welcome opportunity to focus my mind on something beyond my own stress. It wasn't always easy to keep my head in the game. I had to scale back, cancel appointments, rearrange things, and put projects (like this book!) on hold.

My brother survived and as of the writing of this book, he is doing very well. My dad is still in treatment. We've all moved past that month of extreme crisis.

But that time in my life serves as both a warning and an example of how deeply and how quickly disruptions and distractions—and the stress that comes with them—can unravel the work we do. I've already spent a lot of time talking about stress and how it affects us both physically and emotionally, but now I want to talk about distraction. Distraction is a natural response to the stressors in our environment. These stressors can be big things (like my family situation), but more often they are small—as small as the ding of a new message in your inbox.

Most of us have excessive distractions that keep us from our work—phones buzzing in the background, a pop-up on our screen every time someone likes our posts on Facebook or Twitter, the ping-ping-ping of Slack. Sometimes our to-do list is just as distracting as everything else, as we struggle with the distraction of looking at the things we have to do and figuring out what to do next. Add those to the distractions that come from our relationships—kids, and co-workers popping their heads into our offices—and it makes it pretty darn hard to get things done.

Big and small, these distractions wreak havoc on productivity and deeply affect how entrepreneurs work. In this chapter, I will look at some of the most common types of distractions and give you simple tips on how to move past them so that you can stay focused and productive.

SOLVING BIG PROBLEMS

There comes a time in every single founder's life when a big problem comes up. Maybe it's a huge shipping deadline where a perfect product must be ready to go out to customers, but the product isn't ready. Or perhaps there's a problem with the code and hundreds of customers are calling in to troubleshoot an issue. Or it could be a snag in a book contract, a mix-up at a conference, or an issue with human resources. Or perhaps, as in my story above, there's a personal or family crisis that demands center stage for a period of time.

These things happen—to everyone—and while it's never fun to have a big problem, it's also part of owning a business. When big problems happen, everything about your normal day-to-day business should change, and you should go into crisis mode. In crisis mode, things get done. Problems get solved. And you get back on track.

Here are a few tips for operating in crisis mode:

- **Set your micro-goals and checkpoints aside.** A big crisis or problem often pulls your work off from the path of your goals—and it should! Allow yourself the freedom to stop working toward your goals while the problem is solved. Set them aside. Stop your checkpoints. Give yourself some leeway on your micro-goals. Then pour everything into solving the problem. When the problem is solved and the crisis is averted, then you can go right back to where you left off and begin working toward your goals again.

- **Get creative with your work schedule.** Obviously, when a work crisis happens, you will be working much more than you normally would. You likely will stay late in the office, arrive early, even work on days when you normally wouldn't work. When a personal crisis happens, your work schedule may change in the other direction—a few hours here and there. This schedule can be really stressful, especially if you have family and friends counting on you. I have a friend who was on a really tight deadline for a launch of a product, so she began setting her alarm for 3:00 a.m. She would get a cup of coffee and work for two hours while the rest of her family was asleep, and then head back for a couple more hours of sleep before her kids woke up. While this clearly isn't sustainable over a long period of time, for a few days, it allowed her some extra, uninterrupted work time.

- **Get away.** If you feel like the stress of being at home or in an office is stifling your ability to problem-solve, consider getting away. One founder I know checked herself into a hotel for three days and lived on room service as she worked to solve a tough tech problem with one of her apps.

- **Call in the troops.** Calling in extra help—whether it's your mother-in-law to help manage the house or your old college roommate to help re-code an app—can make a huge difference. Be willing to ask for help when you're in crisis mode (and be ready to return the favor and help others when their crisis strikes, too).

- **Allow yourself a regrouping when the crisis is over.** When you have to solve a big problem, that fight-or-flight, acute stress kicks in. This is a good thing—all that extra adrenaline helps you to get things done. But remember how chronic, long-term stress can cause major health issues? That's why it's so important to get out of high-stress mode and back into your normal flow as soon as the crisis is over. So, once you've solved your problem, allow yourself a few days to regroup, to refocus, and to relax. Maybe get away or spend some time away from work, connect with your family in a new way, go on a long walk or bike ride—whatever it takes to restore your spirit and focus to where it was before.

I want to finish this section with a little pep talk: Big problems happen. In every business and to every founder. And when they do happen, they are not a result of a failure on your part, but instead a normal part of being an entrepreneur. So solve that problem with all of the creativity and ingenuity that you can muster, learn from it, and then move forward; get back on track, and keep moving toward those big macro-goals.

TIME, ENERGY, AND ATTENTION

Last February really rocked my ability to push my business forward. As a family, Rob and I have been through several seasons of major disruption. To name a few: Rob trying to keep running Drip while negotiating an acquisition, me trying to finish my dissertation while caring for a newborn, the situation with my dad's and my brother's illnesses. As I said above, disruptions are an inevitable part of a founder's life.

Although I wouldn't choose to go through these challenging seasons, they've been powerful teachers about how to really double down and work well with limited time and an onslaught of distractors. One of the things that disruptions have taught me is that while most of us focus on time management as the key to productivity, it is actually only one of the things that matter. Attention and energy impact productivity just as much as time management does. When time is scarce, and distractions are many, it can be really helpful to target energy and attention.

I'm reading a book called *The Productivity Project* by Chris Bailey and the subtitle is "Accomplishing More by Managing Your Time, Attention, and Energy." Bailey spent a year experimenting with all of the tips, tricks, and hacks that he heard about productivity and distraction.

He took it really far—he went without sleep, he slept too much, he tried working 90-hour weeks and then tried working 20-hour weeks. He tried starting the day with a triple caramel macchiato and he tried going without caffeine (can you imagine?). He basically did a huge, year-long productivity experiment on himself and recorded the data for this book.

After all of his research, Bailey comes to some pretty interesting conclusions about productivity and distraction. His findings echo my own experiences of needing to focus on attention and energy in times of significant disruption. Bailey explains that many people know what equates to an armada of time management tools and techniques, but have no idea how to manage or increase their attention and energy. When this happens, they have the time set aside to sit in front of a computer and work, but no ability to pay attention to that work or energy to focus on it. Their productivity is almost as if they hadn't set the time aside to work at all.

This conclusion makes a lot of sense to me as a psychologist, but also to me as a human, a mother, and an author. I believe every one of us can think back to a time when we stared at a blank Word document for hours trying to get words on paper or stared wide-eyed at a screen trying to solve a problem without really seeing the issue. That's because we had the time, but we didn't have the attention and energy to make that time productive. In the midst of a crisis or crunch time, there's no time for the blank stare.

How do you optimize energy and attention? In his book, Bailey gives founders 20 tips to balance time, energy, and attention. You'll have to read the book to get all of them, but I did want to highlight a few of the tips here that have worked for me.

Tip 1: Start your day with five minutes of meditation.

In the morning, I set my timer for five minutes and sit in silence and focus on my breathing. Five minutes seems like a small amount of time, but it can really make a profound difference in focus and attention. Logically, it makes a lot of sense that if you want your brain to be able to focus and fully engage with a task, it will need periods of deep rest. Meditation is allowing your brain to saturate in oxygen and nutrients while not working very hard and giving it rest so that it is able to focus and engage later in the day.

Tip 2: Choose three things.

Another seems-small-but-is-really-huge idea from Bailey is to write down three things you need to get done each day, then be mindful of those three tasks throughout the day, even as other things begin to distract you. Often, when we get into the office or into work mode, we become inundated with new tasks—an email pops up, a phone call comes in, a new task shows up—and we suddenly get distracted from the big things we need to be doing. So writing down three big things each day—and focusing on them while pushing all other tasks to other days or other times—can really help you to focus on the things you need to get done.

Tip 3: Reset your to-do list.

Every month or two, spend a day giving yourself a "reset." It's so easy to get just a tiny bit off track from where we truly want to be, so spending a day in a mini-retreat or giving ourselves a reset will call us back to focus on the tasks that are beneficial in helping us to be productive in working toward our goals. So spend a day (or even an hour) looking at your big goals and at your to-do list and making sure they align.

Tip 4: Be willing to shift your strategy.

There have been times in my life when I was immersed in a project and it made sense for me work late into the night. But during this most recent family health crisis, my energy plummeted by the end of the day. I also needed to be available to attend medical appointments and help with phone calls to offices open only during traditional business hours. Any highly focused work needed to happen between 6 and 8 a.m., so I shifted everything else back, knowing that the early morning hours were the only thing that I could protect.

Tip 5: Be kind to yourself.

I mentioned this in the last chapter, but it is worth saying twice. It's easy to lose heart or faith as an entrepreneur—especially after a long, unproductive day, or in the midst of a crisis. Perhaps your time was stolen by a bunch of problems, or your energy was sapped by a late night, or you were distracted. Maybe you tried a few strategies and tips and maybe they didn't work out. You start to feel discouraged and unproductive, which, in essence, causes you to be less productive. When you're feeling this way, don't let these emotions steal your productivity. Instead, be kind. Remind yourself that you had a tough day or week, but that you can get better, then push it aside and give yourself a redo the next day.

Because there is always time to improve, always a chance to start over, and always a day when you can get more productive. I think that's what I want to leave you with in regard to Bailey's productivity project. It's a project. Not a to-do list, not a set of rules, not a must-do trick. Instead, it's something you can work on slowly, you can test out, you can adapt, and you can make work for you so that your productivity increases. And in doing so, you will form habits that ultimately make you a more productive and effective founder.

THE LITTLE TASKS THAT ARE KILLING THE BIG TASKS

As an entrepreneur, it is unlikely that you have a job that requires you to work quickly and mindlessly. There are jobs like that—think of the factory jobs during the industrial revolution or agricultural workers harvesting a large field—but as a founder, you likely don't work in that type of field. (Not to mention that in the past several decades, quick mindless jobs have decreased steadily as we as a population have moved into cities and taken on more high-tech jobs.) For most (if not all) entrepreneurs, our work requires clear thoughts and high-quality creativity instead of just "getting a lot of stuff done."

Even with this fact in mind, it's so easy to fall into the trap of spinning in small whirlwind circles trying to get a bunch of little tasks done. We refresh our inboxes again and again, we reply to tweets that have nothing to do with the task at hand, we check Facebook, we update our Trello boards, and by the end of the day, we've gotten a bunch of stuff done—but not the things we needed to get accomplished.

This "little task productivity" actually becomes almost an addiction, if you will. Those feel-good productivity neurons keep firing and firing, and you feel like you're getting a whole lot done, which makes you want to get more done, and then you keep working on the tiny things and never get to the big things.

Deep Work by Cal Newport is another "productivity" book that has guided my thinking. Newport describes deep work as the state of being "all in" on a work task—it is when you are challenged, absorbed, and really working hard to learn something, ship something, or solve a complex problem. This kind of work is extremely satisfying and happens only in the absence of distractions. Deep work must be both cultivated and protected. (If you want to learn more, make sure to pick up the book at CalNewport.com.)

My suggestion is to start by setting aside a big chunk of time (preferably first thing in the morning when you are fresh, or one full day a week when you clear your calendar). Dedicate this time to big tasks—thinking through marketing strategy and writing copy, finishing a chapter per week on your next book, or architecting a new feature for your product. During this time, put your to-do list away, turn off your email, turn off Skype, sign out of Slack, put your phone in the drawer (or lock it in a safe), and focus entirely on your big, creative, important projects. Then set aside a small chunk of time—maybe 20 minutes—to do little tasks so you can get that productivity endorphin rush. Then start again with the time dedicated to the big tasks.

This strategy works, as it allows you to be dedicated to work on the things you need, but still gives you that neuron-firing, feel-good feeling of checking things off your to-do list and keeping your fingers in the details of what your team is doing.

TAKE BACK YOUR INBOX

Email sanity (or shall I say insanity) is one of the biggest thieves of deep work, especially for big-picture leaders like entrepreneurs. The reason is simple: Email—which is ultimately a communication tool built to enhance the ability to communicate and essentially increase productivity—often does just the opposite, as it gives your brain constant reminders of more things you have to do. Imagine you're working on a big marketing plan, a plan that encompasses an entire six-month launch of the product you plan to ship in just a few weeks. The plan has to be thoughtful, compelling, creative, and... done. Yes, before you can ship, you have to be *done*.

Yet, even as you work, you're getting pinged, pinged, pinged with less-important but more-pressing tasks on your email and, before you know it, it's 5 p.m. and you've gotten less than a page of your plan sorted out. That's the power of email. And it's why you have to take back your inbox so it can work for you instead of stealing your productivity.

All that said, I want to emphasize that there is no one "right" way to manage an inbox. I know lots of founders who have different strategies and none are right or wrong, but simply what work for them. The key here is to have *any* strategy—one you have tried, honed, and made sure works for you. This strategy may change during the course of your career, depending on your current productivity needs, the volume of email, the tendency for "fires" to come through your inbox, and a variety of other factors, but the important thing is to have one.

Rob has a strategy that he has honed to help him counter the sheer volume of emails that he gets. His strategy involves two folders in his inbox with the labels "today" and "this week." When he gets an email, he reads it quickly. He calls this his "first pass triage." If it will take less than five minutes to respond, he responds right away so that it's done and gone out of his inbox. If it's something that must be done today, he moves it into "today" and makes sure he gets to it by the end of the day. If it goes into the "this week" folder, he ignores it until he reaches the two-hour block of time that he dedicates on his calendar each week to respond to that box. There is a fourth category of email for him, and these are the big, drawn-out tasks that come in through email. These he forwards on to his Trello board and then puts them into the queue of his to-do list.

This strategy works for him. If you think it might work for you, feel free to try it. Another entrepreneur I know has a virtual assistant—she saves herself hours a week as her assistant goes through her inbox and answers 90% of the questions. Another founder friend sets aside an hour each day to go through her email inbox and after that turns off email for the rest of the day.

Whatever you do, I want to encourage you to have a strategy. Make email work for you so it doesn't steal your time and create unnecessary distraction. Find a system that works, stick to it, adapt it if necessary, and make sure that you use email to your advantage and not disadvantage.

YOGA FOR COMBATING DISTRACTION

One of the things that most helped me survive the crisis period of my family's health problems was to actively work to control the effects of acute stress. I tried to counterbalance the deleterious effects of acute stress by practicing yoga every day. Yoga helps me to create a calm mind while also increasing flexibility and strength in my physical body. It's been so important to my personal well-being that I've actually started teaching yoga at the clinic where I work and using yoga as an adjunctive anxiety treatment.

There's a lot of research behind it as a really powerful tool for helping to monitor anxiety and improve mood, and it's beginning to be widely used for posttraumatic stress disorder (PTSD), anxiety disorders, and depression. Bessel van der Kolk is a psychiatrist and researcher affiliated with Harvard Medical School. His laboratory has done a series of research studies with folks that have PTSD and other trauma-related mental health difficulties. They broke the participants into three groups. One group did an eight-week yoga practice, the second group took standard anti-anxiety medicine, and the third group was a control group. The yoga proved to be more effective than the medicine.

Yoga has been really fun for me—and really beneficial. Yoga has lots of layers, so there's always a new challenge to tackle and a new thing to practice. In my work, the payoff or the outcomes can take months or years, and I don't always know if my clients will get better. In yoga, I get instant gratification in 20 minutes; a session that's a little longer, and I'm learning a new skill in a way that I can see and feel the difference in my head and my body. So it's nice to have something in my life where I can really quickly see the benefits.

One of the ways that yoga works is to help stabilize heart rate. Those of us that run a little anxious have highly variable heart rates, so the emphasis on breath and on calm, strong body movements can be a powerful way to help stabilize and reintegrate steady heart rate and breathing. Yoga is being offered in hospitals and cancer centers, and is becoming well accepted as an important piece of mental well-being and physical well-being.

Yoga may not be the right solution for everyone in times of acute stress—but I do believe that some sort of intentional physical engagement will help every single human. There's a body of research that examines the benefits of exercise for relieving stress (and distraction) for everyone across the board. So find something that resonates with you and use it to drive away that stress. It may mean running through the forest near your house, or it may mean being in the garage on your elliptical watching *Shark Tank* or *The Walking Dead*.

One more thing about exercise or yoga as a relief for stress and the distraction it causes: Make sure your exercise is down time—time when you're not thinking about work or the stressors in your life. Choose something complex or strenuous enough to engage your full mind. When you're thinking about all of the things that are causing stress, it quickly becomes exhausting and will take away the benefits of exercise and turn it into yet another stressor. Instead, clear your mind; allow yourself to meditate or focus on your health, your balance, and your body; and push those stressors aside for a few minutes. Clearing your mind will get you moving in the direction toward your best self and hopefully will help you to refocus and reset—even as you're going through the stress of launching and managing work and being a founder and having a family and everything else.

FINDING THE BALANCE

I remember a time when I was feeling really down about my work. I felt like every day was full of distraction, making it so that I was unproductive and ineffective. I stopped and did a quick assessment and realized that there really wasn't any major stress or urgency right at that moment to get everything done. I wasn't under any major deadlines, yet somehow I had contrived this feeling inside of me that I was in a big hurry to get everything done.

I made the intentional decision to let things be a little easier—to just take my time and work slowly and steadily, and not allow stress to consume my work the entire time I was doing it. Interestingly, this mind shift of allowing myself space to work gave me the ability to focus and increased my productivity. I was able to focus better, feel more energized, and work more effectively, which took the burden of productivity off of my shoulders and, ironically, made me more productive.

And you can do the same. Step back for a minute. Clear your mind. Find ways to give yourself the time, energy, and focus you need to get your productivity back on track, and to get into the flow to get good work done.

9

When Things aren't Getting Done

I think we've all heard the stats: More than 50% of businesses fail in the first five years. (You can read about the entire study at https://www.bls.gov.)

Just reading those words is enough to make most people race out to find a time card to punch. For many, the idea of venturing into something that risky and that prone to failure is simply out of the question. They aren't willing or able to pour their life, their work, their passion, their money, and their time into something that has a likely chance of failing.

But not entrepreneurs.

I'm guessing the entrepreneurs reading this are thinking they like those odds. Men and women who value freedom, ingenuity, adventure, and meaning see that while there is a 50% chance of failure, there is also a 50% chance of success. With that success comes freedom and adventure, the opportunity for more ingenuity, and, eventually, meaning. It's worth the risk to them.

There's also a whole lot more to those stats than meets the eye. A 2014 Gallup poll confirmed that yes, indeed, more than 50% of businesses fail in their first five years. But there's more: The businesses that do succeed have a major commonality. It's not funding or cash flow. It's not geographical location or technology. It's not even growth or monetization. Instead, based on a poll of more than 4,000 businesses in the U.S. and Canada, the one thread that tied successful businesses to each other was completely unexpected: It was the entrepreneur.

No, all of these businesses didn't share the same founder, but instead, each of their founders shared similar values and personality traits. Basically, they had the tenacity, intelligence, creativity, passion, and drive to help their businesses succeed.

Now I've put a whole lot of pressure on you, haven't I? I hope not. Because the truth is, the mere fact that you are reading this book means that you consider yourself an entrepreneur and that you value things like freedom, ingenuity, adventure, and meaning, which means that you are already halfway there. But what happens if that's not enough? What happens if your business starts to struggle?

BURNOUT

Every single entrepreneur I know goes through periods where they've lost their oomph.

Often, it's due to a struggling business. Perhaps that growth curve has stagnated (or flatlined) or the feedback you're getting is that your product is all wrong. Perhaps your team is in conflict. Perhaps your expansion has failed, and you're having to go through layoffs or cutbacks, or stop the growth of a new division. Maybe everything is going fine, but you've reached a point of exhaustion. It's easy to feel defeated or burned out at that point.

But other times, that oomph goes away for different reasons. One friend of mine found herself without the oomph to keep going because her business had succeeded. She had spent years pursuing financial freedom, and when she finally reached it, she felt like she lost her drive. Her purpose was gone. Another friend of mine felt like his business had gone in a new—and very successful—direction, but that new direction didn't align with his strengths.

A more formal term for "losing your oomph" is burnout. The concept was developed by Christina Maslach, a professor of social psychology at UC Berkeley. She talks about burnout as a state of chronic stress that leads to:

- Physical and emotional exhaustion
- Cynicism and detachment
- Feelings of ineffectiveness and lack of accomplishment

Burnout is not depression, and it isn't a simple result of long hours. Burnout is no longer caring, no longer having energy, and no longer feeling like our efforts matter. It is sustained exhaustion and deflation. The recipe for burnout is chronic stress without social support, without meaningful goals, and without much control over how we carry out our work.

Burnout makes us suck at our work. It is toxic to productivity, creativity, complex problem-solving, interpersonal relationships, and motivation. If you're serious about shipping, you simply can't afford burnout in yourself or your team. I'm not saying this lightly, either—there is solid, tested research that shows that burnout can greatly affect productivity for any individual.

Researchers have shown that burnout has the power to change the function, structure, and chemistry of the brain. Researchers looked at neuroimaging of the brains of folks who were feeling burned out and found that they had enlarged amygdalae, which is the part of the brain that regulates negative feelings like fear and anxiety. Additionally, the imaging showed decreased connections between the amygdalae and the anterior cingulate cortex, which is the part of the brain that regulates emotional distress.

These small structural changes can cause people to feel a heightened level of negative emotions and then have a hard time calming down from those feelings, causing the cycle to spiral further and further over time. This cycle can lead to struggles in productivity, but also in memory, attention, and anxiety.

If brain changes aren't enough to freak you out about burnout, a team of researchers at Tel Aviv Sourasky Medical Center (https://www.ncbi.nlm.nih.gov/pubmed/23006431) tracked health screenings of 8,838 employees for an average of 3.4 years. They found that people who demonstrated high levels of burnout had a 79% higher risk of being diagnosed with heart disease over the course of the study. Yikes!

Unfortunately, for most, burnout creeps up slowly and in a way that is easy to miss and easy to ignore. Many entrepreneurs don't realize they are dealing with burnout until it is already affecting their productivity. It starts with a high-stress, high-impact job. This stressful environment coupled with low social support, no clear or meaningful goals, too much work, few observable successes, and limited control causes burnout. A mismatch between what we think is important and the demands of our workday quickly creeps in, and burnout begins.

I think entrepreneurs are particularly susceptible to burnout because many of us work alone or on small teams. As a group, we tend to value personal freedom and control so much that we are vulnerable to deep discouragement and frustration when confronting problems that are beyond our control.

Ironically, many of the most burned-out entrepreneurs I know are very successful. Their companies are growing, but the growth is taking them away from their competence and their sweet spots (the life of a CEO running a 15-person team is very different than the life of a freelancer or solopreneur or someone running a team of three carefully selected people). To go from freelancer to CEO in two years is a popular dream, but it may be a recipe for burnout.

If we go back to those core values of entrepreneurs—freedom, ingenuity, adventure, and meaning—we can make the assumption that a founder will lose that oomph when those values aren't being met in their lives. Likewise, part of the nature of running a start-up or business is that there will be times when you will lose your freedom, when your sense of ingenuity is stifled, or when the adventure starts to feel monotonous and your meaning is muted by the stress of your business. So, with some simple A + B = C math, it becomes pretty obvious that every entrepreneur will face burnout at some point in her career.

So what do you do about it?

1. Celebrate successes.
Take time to honor what is going well. Because burnout can shift the way that your brain functions, it can be easy to focus only on the downside. Intentionally practice noticing the wins, the progress, the growth, and the high points in your business. This helps to counterbalance that overactive amygdala.

2. Define your goals.
Clear, focused goals allow us to celebrate success. Because a big part of burnout is *feeling like* you're not accomplishing anything, segmenting

your work into small, clear, achievable goals can help bring a reality check to your biased view that nothing is getting done. In addition, our brains get a little jolt of happy endorphins when we experience the success of finishing something. This also helps counteract that overactive amygdala. Not sure how to make goal setting a meaningful part of your work life? I interviewed a bunch of successful founders about how they do it. Check out ZenFounder.com podcast episodes 51-56.

3. *Quit doing things that suck the life out of you.*
No one is able to spend a lot of time doing something they don't care about—time on the hamster wheel makes anyone, but especially an entrepreneur, feel depressed and burned out. So once you find your strengths and passions, stop doing the things that aren't in that wheelhouse. Or at least stop doing them so much.

One founder friend had a small business that was really thriving. Everything seemed to be going well—revenue was pouring in, his product was getting rave reviews, his team was growing—but he felt like he was ready to give up. He was so burned out that he had trouble getting up in the morning and the idea of going into his office felt daunting. He began to wonder if he should sell his business and go back to his old 9 to 5 job.

After some careful contemplation, though, he realized that his exhilaration and drive came from time spent problem-solving. He loved coming up with solutions and technology that helped other businesses thrive. What he didn't love was the day-to-day management of the office: HR, insurance, lawyers.... He isn't a gifted administrator, and the idea of running an actual business made him feel completely burnt out.

The simple solution was that he hired a manager to run the day-to-day aspects of his business so he could hole-up with the development team and create. He got that oomph back, and his business continued to thrive.

4. *Rest.*
When you feel like you've lost that oomph, the solution is not to keep pressing forward. Burnout is your body and soul telling you that you need a break. It may be time for a vacation or a sabbatical. Continuing to push

once you've reached the point of burnout will only solidify the negative patterns and dangerous physiological changes. Take time to re-evaluate and ask yourself some deeper questions.

At minimum, go on a retreat. Let yourself step away from the urgent to evaluate the important. Not sure how to get started? Here's our guide: https://gumroad.com/l/retreats.

The good news is that it is absolutely possible to recover from burnout, even on a neurological level. But you have to rest.

5. Connect

We are a social species. We can't thrive in isolation. Burnout is inherently isolating- part of burnout is detachment from customers, colleagues, and loved ones. The only road back is to counteract the isolation by deciding to pursue connection. Easier said than done. Masterminds and entrepreneurs groups are a great way to get started. You are not alone in your struggles with burnout.

In order to make connecting easy, we created ZenTribes. These are groups of 6-8 entrepreneurs who join together for focused conversation about how to stay sane and healthy in the midst of the ups and downs of business life. Whether you join one of our tribes or find your way to another community. Connection is a necessary part of burnout prevention and burnout recovery.

6. Stick to what is most meaningful

The last suggestion is to stop and ask the big question. *Why* are you doing what you are doing? What is the *meaning* that drives your business? We can do hard things when we believe those things are meaningful. Burnout can signal that you've moved too far from the meaning that originally motivated you. Or perhaps life has changed and the meaning that once drove you is no longer relevant. It's time to go back to the drawing board and re-evaluate what is most important to you right now.

Burnout is common. And it is terrible. The good news is that it is possible to recover from.

KNOWING WHEN TO QUIT

You know that whole Winston Churchill thing about never, ever, ever giving up? Well, it's wrong. What we should be saying is never, ever, ever give up *quickly*. But there are times in every entrepreneur's life when giving up is the right thing to do.

Rob's company Drip is one of the leading marketing automation apps right now and has tens of thousands of users, but in its beginning stages, there were times that Rob wondered if it was ever going to succeed. In its first year, Drip was pretty stagnant in its growth. I remember Rob coming home feeling pretty defeated and telling me he was worried that Drip (an idea he really believed in) was about to flatline.

You've had days like this, too, haven't you?

Every entrepreneur has.

And I want to start out by telling you that if there wasn't that tension between risk and success, if every idea you had automatically soared, if you never experienced failure, then you wouldn't be an entrepreneur at all. After all, the heart of entrepreneurship is based on creativity and ingenuity and throwing ideas into the world to see if they fly.

Failure is always a real possibility.

And so, the question is: How long do you pursue an idea or business before you throw in the towel?

The answer is that there is no real answer, but instead, many different variables that you can use to gauge whether to quit. With Drip, Rob said that he believed in the idea so much, and had invested so much time and energy and money into it, that he intended to push forward until it either worked or until he knew that it had absolutely no chance of working.

So how do you know when to give up? Here are the questions to ask yourself:

1. Is there some form of growth, even if it's not revenue growth?

Even during Drip's darkest days, Rob had signs of hope that it had potential. His revenue wasn't growing, but he had a strong group of early adopters who were giving him positive feedback on the app. Additionally, based on some customer polling and research, he received promises that more customers would come if he built certain features that were on the cutting edge of marketing automation.

Rob took a risk: He bet the farm, so to speak, that if he built those new features, people would come. In hindsight, it was a good risk, but it was also an informed risk. Rob didn't just risk the failure of the company (not to mention loads of time and money) on an idea that he had. He used the early data from Drip—data that said customers liked the product and wanted more—to inform his decision to take the risk.

Before you give up on a struggling business, spend some time looking beyond the simple numbers and into the other factors that indicate growth. Look at customer feedback, customer reviews, a market that indicates a need for your product in the near future, or a variety of other factors that indicate a potential for growth.

2. Have I worked with trusted advisors?

Rob works with four other entrepreneurs in a mastermind group. These people are all like-minded businessmen who spend time every month helping each other's businesses succeed. Rob said that the second he worries a business or idea is struggling, he takes the data—growth, revenue, feedback, etc.—straight to his masterminds group for careful analysis. They look things over with him, ask the tough questions, and give him ideas on how to push through. They also are willing to tell him if it's time to give up.

Every great entrepreneur has a group of mentors and advisors behind them. So the first place you need to go when you're feeling not so great is to the people who have been there to support you, advise you, and help you from the beginning. I do need to warn you here that there is a possibility that your advisors will tell you that it's time to give up, time to quit. And this can really sting. But having advisors who are willing to ask the tough questions and tell you the truth about your business is the key to success, as well as the key to avoiding future failure.

3. Have I stepped off the emotional roller coaster?

When I was a junior in college, I spent a year studying in Ghana, West Africa. The first months were amazing. I was curious about everything around me. I traveled constantly, pushing myself to experience the vastness and excitement of increasingly "off-the-beaten-path" and remote places. I lived on adrenaline and adventure. I met amazing people, encountered just a bit of danger, and felt like I was falling in love with the very red clay earth under my feet. But after months of bucket baths, hitchhiking, and a diet consisting mostly of yam and goat, I began to get tired, lonely, and homesick. I lost my oomph. My high highs had turned into low lows.

The same goes for business. When you're on fire with a new idea, it can consume you. You spend every waking minute considering how to make it better, how to be more successful, how to move forward. And you likely show some great early success. But then something happens. A problem with your product. A mistake in your app. A disgruntled customer. And the motivation disappears. What was once all-consuming starts to feel daunting and overwhelming. You lose your oomph.

Don't give up purely because you are frustrated, because you have lost your motivation, or because you are seeing some signs of failure. Instead, step off that roller coaster and look at it with a detached eye. Emotional highs and emotional lows are not great moments for big decisions. Find emotional homeostasis before making a huge decision. This process may require some help from your trusted advisors or your family, as they will be able to look at the situation from a more objective viewpoint.

4. Have I moved beyond the sunk cost fallacy?

One of the reasons many entrepreneurs don't want to give up on their business is the sunk cost fallacy. Basically, they have already sunk so much time, energy, and money into the business that the idea of walking away feels like a huge waste. But giving up on a business is not a waste if the business was never going to succeed—and the time, energy, and money that was sunk into that failed business is not wasted, either. Remember the basic values of an entrepreneur: freedom, ingenuity, adventure, and meaning.

Notice that words like "money" and "success" and "accolades" aren't on that list.

Even a failed business can bring an entrepreneur closer to her core values. Even a failed business can bring freedom. An idea that flatlines serves to fuel future ingenuity. The ups and downs of a start-up bring adventure. And the meaning that comes from trying something new, from creating something, from pushing the boundaries, comes regardless of whether the business succeeds.

5. Have I thought about it for long enough?

There were times in the early days of Drip when Rob came home and told me that Drip was going to fail. He was in turmoil. He believed in his idea, he thought it could succeed, he had positive feedback, but it simply wasn't growing like he expected. Those were dark days. We spent hours breaking down the app, talking about why it was created in the first place, the ingenuity behind it, and the reasons it wasn't growing.

But notice something: I said there were days. I didn't say there were months. Years. Decades. Had that gone on for longer, I'm not sure that either of us could have emotionally managed it. But the amount of time that Rob struggled with Drip was tenable. It was part of the process for a new app and a new idea. It was a downswing before the upswing.

The question you need to ask yourself is this: How long have I thought this isn't going to work? And then ask yourself how long can you—emotionally, physically, financially, relationally—tolerate the curve?

WHEN YOUR BUSINESS FAILS

Like I said at the beginning of this chapter: Businesses do fail. Some fail right from the start, floundering from day one and eventually fizzling out. But others—and these are the losses that really sting—see moderate success and give the founder a taste of victory before they start to go downhill.

Either way, when you do make the decision to let your business go, it's a huge loss. You likely poured your heart, soul, and mind into your business for months or even years, and when you lose that, it feels like bereavement. If an app has failed or a start-up has folded, you have to end what has ended. What I mean by that is that you can't just set it aside and wake up the next day and move on. It needs to be put to rest, if you will.

The first thing you have to do is honor that loss and how you feel about it. It's almost like having a funeral for your business—you need to say goodbye, honor the time and energy and creativity that was put into it, and put the business to rest.

This process could mean taking some time away to contemplate the business, or potentially talking to a group of other entrepreneurs and having a little bit of a post-mortem on your business. Talk about what failed, why it failed, and how you can learn from that. Ask yourself the questions you need to ask to make sure that you have learned from the experience and can move forward.

My next suggestion is to put your founder's mind to rest for awhile. Step away from work and anything that has to do with your business. Stop listening to tactical start-up podcasts or reading books about founding businesses. Go on a retreat. Consider your strengths. Ease up on the throttle for a few months, and you'll often find that you'll not only get your motivation back, but you'll come back stronger and smarter.

I want to end this section with a reminder: Businesses fail all the time. This doesn't mean you're a failure or you don't have what it takes to be a founder. So, allow yourself time to reflect and learn, but remember the values that drove you to be a founder to begin with: freedom, ingenuity, adventure, and meaning. Those values are deep-seated and likely still hold true to your spirit, so cling to those.

And then go out and try, try again.

WHAT'S NEXT?

I want to finish this chapter by talking about hunger.

One of the things that makes a founder's mindset so great is that entrepreneurs are hungry. They are hungry to pursue their core values—and then to move beyond them. And whether you have founded a business that barely gets by or one that has recurring revenue that far exceeds your lifestyle, I want to remind you to stay hungry.

My advice is to always strive for freedom first. Make sure you have the money in the bank to get yourself through tough patches and the flexibility in your schedule to make it through busy times. But once you've done that, strive for purpose. Find out what drives you beyond just freedom and money. This is the art of nonconformity—it's how you can leave a legacy of thinking bigger and better about so many things.

I love the concept of "hungry" because it defines the drive that all founders innately have. That said, beyond money and freedom, what's next for you may be a "new version of hunger." Maybe you become hungry for other businesses to thrive and start angel investing or mentoring other founders. Maybe that hunger is for creativity, so you start working toward a new invention or expanding your current products. Maybe that hunger is for family and adventure, so you begin deepening your relationships.

For many founders, the "what's next" involves a longing for the pursuit. You want to be excited about work again, and you need something new and big to move forward on. This need is why it's so important to have fluidity in what your definition of success is. Monetary success isn't necessarily success. That moment of arrival—when you know your business is going to make it and thrive—isn't necessarily success. (Or if it is, that success isn't static or permanent.) Yes, these things are important and should be celebrated, but trust me when I tell you that your feeling of "success" will last only a short time. Be prepared for that, and then allow your mind to grow hungry for what's next.

What's next may be a new company.

It may be a reorganization of the old one.

It may be personal growth with your relationships or your family.

It may be time to hang out with your kids or grandkids.

But whatever it is, whatever you've been through, wherever you're going, you'll fail only when you stop being hungry for what's next.

10

Staying Connected

Why do you need others in order to be a successful founder? After all, it was your idea, your invention, your spark of ingenuity that started everything, and it was on your shoulders that the business was built. Why can't you be the one to continue to carry that business as it moves forward? It's you and your idea against the world, and why shouldn't it be? You can carry it forward on your own, make it thrive, and get it all done before next quarter. Superfounder to the rescue!

It's ironic to read that last paragraph because it is so contradictory to everything any of us have ever read about successful business practices. I think we all believe, in theory, that we can't carry the entire load of a business on our own, and we certainly can't build a successful business without support, collaboration, and partnership. But when reality sets in, most of us tend to hunker down, put on our superhero cape, and act like we don't need anything from anybody. This is crazy. I can tell you without hesitation that the you-against-the-world mindset won't make you happy, and it won't make your company more successful.

Freedom, autonomy, adventure, and creativity are among the key values that drive entrepreneurs and, to be honest, those aren't traits that lead people to be particularly oriented toward sustaining close relationships. To the do-it-yourselfer, the idea of relying or depending on others feels foreign or unnecessary. That, coupled with the fact that being a founder is all-consuming, means the drift toward isolation isn't difficult.

Isolation and loneliness happen so slowly for most founders that it's hard to identify. They spend years in start-up mode: head down, solving problems, building, moving forward, and before they realize what has happened, they're suffering. Big issues like divorces, rifts between parents and children, and the dissolution of business partnerships seem to almost pop up out of nowhere. Then people are hurt and businesses are destroyed.

But the hurt goes deeper than that, even. Your mental health is deeply affected by your relationships. When things aren't talked through, collaborated on, and discussed, all of those common founder emotions like frustration, hopelessness, loneliness, and anxiety get bottled up inside, eventually exploding in anger or resulting in distraction and burnout. It's just not good for you or your business to be alone.

Yet so many founders find themselves feeling completely isolated and lonely. It's a big—huge, prevalent—problem in the entrepreneurial world. A problem with far-reaching consequences. A problem with a very simple solution: Founders must (absolutely *must*) be intentional about having strong relationships with people in their lives. Ironically, one of the best ways to build personal connections is to have a healthy, strong relationship with your business.

You can have a successful business and stay connected to others in a very real and very meaningful way. But it takes intentional steps. In this chapter, I'm going to talk about the people that founders do (and should) depend on for support, and then I'm going to help you to figure out how to best connect with each group in a healthy, beneficial way. But first, we are going to start with how to have a healthy relationship with your business.

YOUR BUSINESS IS NOT YOUR BABY

As I mentioned in Chapter 4, I recently read a research study published in Human Brain Mapping that compared brain scans (fMRIs) of fathers thinking about their children to brain scans of entrepreneurs thinking about their businesses. It may not shock you to learn that the regions of neurological activation were very similar. Both fathers and founders experienced activation in the part of their brain that releases dopamine. This is a reward center—we feel good when it is activated.

Like fathers, gazing at images of their sweet young children, entrepreneurs experienced a little swirl of reward—a little dopamine hit—when gazing at images of their company. At the neurological level, entrepreneurs have a lovey-dovey, affectionate relationship with their company.

In addition, the entrepreneurial brains, like the fathers' brains, demonstrated a suppression of the parts of the brain that are connected to critical social processing. These areas of the brain are important to social assessment or the ability to read and evaluate the intentions of another person. (This is the part of your brain that was active last night at a cocktail party as you scanned the room and unconsciously evaluated who was worth talking to and who would likely be a jerk.)

When these brain areas are offline or suppressed, people are unable to accurately connect with and relate to others. The founders in this study were essentially unable to critically assess their company as a separate entity. Instead, the business was encoded in their brains as an extension of the self. (And just like romantic love and parental love, founder love is blind.)

I had a few different reactions to reading this article.

First, it explained some things about founders to me. Some of it is good: It demonstrates the sacrifice, the drive, the craziness that comes from being a founder. Parental love brings forth the best and worst in human beings. I never knew how patient, self-sacrificing, and strong I could be until I had children. And I never knew how selfish, short-tempered, and crazy I could be until I had children.

The same goes for being a founder: Sometimes you feel obsessed and on-fire. Other times, you are passionate and creative. Often, you are a little irrational about all you're doing to grow your business, and now we know there's some science behind that.

Secondly, this research shows something that you certainly already know: Our businesses are important. Your business is an essential part of your satisfying and meaningful life. How fortunate that we, as entrepreneurs, have created ways to make a living that make our very brains gush. If you find something that provides a living and makes your brain mushy, gushy in love: to hell with the rest—do that!

But I'm also a little bit troubled by the implications of how deeply a business can become integrated with our very being. The suspension of critical assessment is scary to me as a psychologist. Just like in any important human relationship, too much fusion, too much enmeshment, and too many connected emotions can be dangerous. Giving your whole heart to a business (that, by the way, can't love you back) is psychologically dangerous.

I want to help you find the balance between a healthy relationship with the baby that is your business and staying emotionally healthy. I want you to have all of those feel-good, gushy feelings about the ideas you are creating, while still being able to maintain a safe and effective critical distance from your work.

START-UP ATTACHMENT DISORDER (SAD) -OR- BUSINESS ATTACHMENT DISORDER (BAD)

The first sentence of the article was "My name is Jon, and I suffer from start-up attachment disorder."

Talk about a great opening line! I read it and then read it again as I contemplated what Jon Hainstock meant when he wrote that sentence. From a clinical perspective, attachment disorders are pervasive difficulties with experiencing trust and stability in relationships. Jon's post and our subsequent interview (if you want to listen, it's Zen Founder episode 59) became a very helpful way for me to think about a founder's relationship with their business.

Jon struggled heavily for years with what he calls "start-up attachment disorder"—his name for the common tendency of founders to replace their human connections with their business and create an almost second-spouse situation in which the business is the second (or sometimes first!) love. Entrepreneurs can get so emotionally attached to their business that they come to relate to the business as if it were another person. Unfortunately for entrepreneurs, most businesses are not great humanoids to be in love with. They are erratic and demanding, not good listeners, and they never, ever take out the trash. (*No, Rob. I'm not secretly talking about you.*)

Jon and his co-founder worked together on their business—an app-based employee scheduling software called ZoomShift. They weathered a four-year roller coaster of founding the business—pressing forward through an incubator stage where their main investor lost all of his money and had to pull out; a start-up digital agency; a re-emergence of their software; having to self-fund the business as it grew; and simply dealing with every up, down, high, and low that comes with a start-up.

In the first few years of Jon's venture, most days were spent in a problem-come, problem-solved mentality, where the cycle of figuring out the business and pushing it forward occupied most of their emotional energy. Jon pushed through for months, but eventually, it caught up to him. A human can survive in "survival mode" for only so long.

There came a day when that shifted. Jon remembers a moment when he took a step back and looked at the meta-levels of how he was doing and realized things weren't good. He felt these huge swings in his feelings about his venture—one day he would feel like it was the best thing he had ever done, it was going to be his lifestyle business that carried him to retirement, and the next he was ready to sell the whole thing and start over. He loved it. He hated it. Either way, the business was occupying every waking thought, and he began to feel really low—really frustrated and helpless and as if his entire life was hinging on something that was erratic and unpredictable. Jon's start-up had hijacked his life.

If Jon's start-up had been a girlfriend, it might have been easier to see what was happening. Maybe his buddies would have staged an intervention and let him know, over a couple of beers, that the girl wasn't worth the drama. Or that she wasn't really showing him the kind of love that he was offering her. If the start-up had been a girlfriend, maybe Jon would have gotten into therapy, and learned about anxious-preoccupied attachment and fearful-avoidant attachment—both of which are relation-ship styles that are insecure, erratic, and emotionally unhealthy.

But Jon's start-up wasn't a girlfriend. (He is happily married.) His start-up was a business that *felt* like a bad girlfriend.

Jon's start-up held him hostage, and in every single moment his thoughts seemed to toil over his business. Because of this, his business had thrived, but his relationships and his emotional health had not. He talked to his co-founder about it, and they realized together that both of them were struggling with a wide range of troubling emotions around the business. Through a lot of work, they were able to identify where they each were emotionally, and figured out how they could support them-selves and each other in order to take care of their emotional health.

Why did they get to such a low place to begin with?

A business takes over everything. It takes over your time, your energy, your thoughts, and your emotions, and with that comes a weightiness that is always there, no matter what you do. At that point, it's so easy to start telling yourself that you've got it handled, you're doing fine, and you don't need anyone or anything. From there, it's a slow progression to let-ting yourself be more and more consumed by the work. Soon, you wake up, and that's what you think about; when you're with friends and family, that's what you're thinking about; when you go to sleep, that's what you're thinking about.

This is a misplaced identity—the job or the start-up or the idea has become both who the founder is and what the founder loves. But your business simply can't carry the weight of who you are—it will never be your value or your purpose. Nor is it a good love outlet, because it just can't love you back. Your start-up doesn't have the shoulders to bear that weight, and it shouldn't. So that misplaced emotional attachment has to go if you want to be healthy and strong for yourself, for your business, and for your family.

Jon is obviously a very smart, intuitive guy and he is fortunate enough to have a co-founder who clearly understands and stands with him, in addition to a support system made up of his family and friends, which helped him to overcome these struggles before they got too serious. Together, he and his co-founder were able to come up with some strategies that helped them both to move forward with ZoomShift in a way that maintained their emotional health and kept their business strong at the same time. These are a few of the things they did:

1. **Escape the technology.** I have a friend who pays for two iPhones simply so that she can have one for work and one for personal use. She keeps her work contacts and her personal contacts on separate phones. She keeps her work email and personal email on separate phones. And when she leaves the office at the end of each day, she plugs her work phone into a charging station and leaves it at the office. I know this sounds a bit crazy, but her reasoning is that she was finding herself completely chained to her work, even when she was at home eating dinner with her family or watching her kid's soccer games. An inbox notification would pop up, and she felt like she had to answer it. While this option may be too extreme for you, it's good to find a way to escape from work technology when you are with your family and friends so that you can focus completely on them. This may mean leaving your phone in the office, or putting it in a drawer when you're not working, or even turning off notifications. Whatever you decide, make an intentional effort to leave your work communication for your work hours so that you can focus on your relationships.

2. **Never let it become your "other relationship."** Rob and I sometimes joke that Drip is his "other wife." He'll get yet another call from her and step outside during family dinner, or have to run off to the office on a Saturday night to solve an issue. This is often unavoidable for a founder—you will have things that pop up with your business that infringe on your family time or personal time. I'm certainly not telling you to ignore issues that arise—but instead, learn to keep your family and friends abreast of what is developing so that they can partner with you. When Rob says, "Hey, Sherry, I

just got a call from Derrick, and the team is having some trouble with a database migration. I need to help troubleshoot and support the team," then I know exactly what he's doing, where he's going, and how I can support him. It's not an amorphous drift... I am not left wondering whether I got ditched for the other woman. I know what's going on and why it is important.

3. **Focus on both quality time and quantity time.** In our fast-paced, productivity-driven world, we tend to focus on quality time at the expense of quantity time. So when we have only 10 minutes a day to give to our spouse, we assume it's fine as long as we really pay attention to them during those 10 minutes. Not true. Yes, you should spend good, quality time with people, but you have to make time for them, too. You have to give yourself and your relationships the space they need to develop into deep, meaningful relationships. This means different things for different relationships. With your spouse, it may mean setting aside one night a week for date night, while with your business partner, it may mean a weekly lunch out of the office to discuss how you're doing. With your kids, it may mean stationing yourself in the kitchen after school so that you're around for seemingly random but potentially very important comments that happen at the end of the day.

4. **Be present.** The thing about great, meaningful relationships is that they don't happen through osmosis. You can't just sit on a couch next to your spouse or kids and magically learn all there is to know about how they are feeling and doing through osmosis. You have to work on it, and that often starts with being present. My oldest son often needs some "lead time" before he can get deep about his feelings or thoughts. So, if he walks into the kitchen and I'm frantically washing dishes and prepping for dinner, he's probably not going to say much to me. I have to stop, to look at him, to give him my full, undistracted attention, and he will open up and really share with me how he is feeling. When you are with the people you love, stop the other things you are doing

and allow yourself the time to be present and fully invested in that relationship.

5. **Be patient.** Strong relationships don't happen overnight—and this is especially true for relationships that have perhaps been neglected in the past. If you spent months or years suffering from "start-up attachment disorder," if your relationships have been back-burnered for way too long, if you have worked in isolation since the very beginning, it will take time to turn it around. You're taking the first step by intentionally investing in your relationships—good for you—but be patient with yourself and others, as building relationships takes time.

The good news is that start-up attachment disorder is curable. I know many founders who have found the balance between a healthy start-up and healthy relationships. It takes intentionality, hard work, and thoughtful strategies, but with time and effort, you can find balance between your business and the people in your life. Keep moving forward, keep trying, and keep investing, and slowly things will change. Your business won't feel like a crazy boyfriend, and your family won't feel like a distant cast of characters from a movie you used to love.

WHY ARE YOU LONELY WHEN YOU ARE SURROUNDED BY PEOPLE?

One of the most common things I hear from founders is that the people in their lives don't "get it." The spouse, neighbors, college roommate, siblings, and parents don't understand the pressures and challenges of being an entrepreneur.

"No one else gets what it's like to be running *my* business."

"No one understands my day-to-day life and telling them would be a long, arduous process."

"No one else could possibly understand what I'm feeling right now."

"Other people don't have the combination of pressures and responsibilities that I have."

I want to tell you decisively right now that these thoughts are untrue. Your brain is playing a trick on you. It is, of course, true that nobody else in the world has experienced the exact same things that you have experienced. So, on a very minute level, they cannot understand every detail of what you do and how you are feeling. Nobody gets the ins and outs of your job or knows the details of what you do like you do.

But everybody—literally, every single human—has experienced frustration. We've all felt sad. We all know what it's like to be uncertain or scared. Every one of us has felt unmotivated or burned out. All of us have experienced doubt or lack of confidence. We've all felt uncertain about the future or questioned a decision that we've made. And all of us have known the joy of success or the thrill that comes when the pieces of life come together in just the right way. These are universal emotions that everyone has experienced, and yet so many founders feel like they are alone against the world.

You're not alone.

I'll repeat that: You are not alone.

Just like how it's easy to get into the habit of thinking you are alone and living in isolation as a founder, it's also something that can be easily overcome. You just need to get into the habit of saying yes to people. "Yes, I can have coffee just to talk. Yes, I would love to tell you about my day and see if you have any thoughts. Yes, I do want some advice." Yes, yes, yes.

I don't want to minimize the feelings of being alone or misunderstood, because I recognize that they are real feelings, ones that often can lead to depression or anxiety.

But in the kindest, most helpful way, I'd like to tell you "get over yourself. You are not that special." Perhaps it is time to stop trying to be understood and shift gears to focus on understanding. Listen to those around you—listen to their heartaches, annoyances, and fears. Listen to their joys and celebrations. Careful listening will help you to build a bridge between your situation and theirs. Whether you want to connect with your stay-at-home-dad husband, your wife who is an emergency room doctor, your tween-aged daughter, or your retired, golf-obsessed dad—you'll find the point of connection and understanding if you listen well.

Please hear that I am not telling you to deny your own needs for connection and simply don your superhero cape and listen to the worries and burdens of everyone else. No. I am telling you that you'll know how to help your family and friends understand your founder's life by listening for common emotions and worries in the stories of their lives. We are all human, so the best way to connect with others is through those very real, very human emotions.

HAVING A SOUNDING BOARD

Earlier, I wrote about the voices in your head. I explained that each of us has a constant internal feedback loop in our brains, essentially talking us through every step we take in our lives. Our thoughts help us to solve problems, to make decisions, and to get things done. Here's the problem: You can't always trust the voices in your head.

When you're stressed or anxious, or feeling hopeless or unmotivated, those voices start to play a feedback loop that isn't quite accurate. Perhaps those inner voices begin to tell you that success is impossible and your work is futile. Or maybe they blind you to a part of your business that isn't working. Sometimes, they make us feel depressed or despondent, and other times, they bring false, inflated optimism.

If you want to be able to trust the voices in your head—and essentially the decisions that you make as a result of them—you need to have a sounding board. Ultimately, it would be great to have many sounding boards—your spouse, your co-founder, your business partners, your friends—but at the very least, you have to have one. And I recommend that you start with a therapist.

Hold on—don't stop reading. I'm not telling you that you're mentally ill or need your head checked. Just read the next few paragraphs and hear me out on the therapist thing.

I'm very utilitarian about the idea of therapy. We go to the dentist to take care of our teeth and the barber to cut our hair because dentists and barbers have skills and specialized training. They can see angles that we can't see, and spot problems we don't recognize. They know the latest techniques and have the responsibility to help us handle one small part of our lives. Similarly, therapists have years of specialized training in emotional health and inner life and relationships. A good therapist will help you spot potential problems before they blow up and will help you build the emotional resources you need to handle the inevitable ups and downs. They see angles you can't see.

I would love to normalize therapy as part of preventive health—not just something to go to when there is an acute or egregious problem (or when your spouse demands it), but instead a place to go to find a healthy, expert sounding board to help you see your own blind spots, identify negative thinking patterns, and make sure you are on track with your emotional health.

When I was training to become a psychologist, it was a strong recommendation that every person in my cohort go to therapy for at least six months. At first, we wondered aloud what we would talk about to a therapist if there wasn't anything acutely wrong with our emotional health, but we all quickly realized that therapy can be so much more than simply a solution to a problem. Instead, my therapist became my sounding board. A sounding board that helped to support the decisions I was making, endeavored to understand how my past experiences were impacting my professional development and my adult relationships, listened to my answers, and helped me to reflect personally and professionally on how things were going.

In a perfect world, I would recommend that every founder establish a relationship with a therapist right at the point that they start their business. I suggest that you go weekly for a few months and establish a relationship with a therapist that is known and trusted. And then, I would suggest that you use that therapist as a sounding board—as needed—as the business grows. Maybe you go once a week, or once a month, or just when you're feeling that something isn't quite right.

My friend, Cory Miller, the founder of iThemes, has been very public about the important role that therapy has played in his business and personal life. His first marriage ended several years ago, and he spiraled down into a deep depression, despite his successful and growing company. He began seeing a therapist to help knit him back together. Now, many years later, his therapist, Kyle, is available for a check-in whenever Cory needs one. It is an important relationship in which Cory can talk about the things that worry him, the difficulties he might be having with his team, his customers, or his family members; it's a place to talk about the future and what might be next.

Let go of whatever you think you know about therapy—it doesn't have to be boxes of tissues or lying prostrate on a chaise lounge. It can be a life-changing relationship. Definitely consider adding a mental health professional to your repertoire of helpful relationships.

GOAL ACCOUNTABILITY AND MASTERMINDS

We talked a bit about the theme of accountability when we discussed goal checkpoints, so I want to spend a bit of time here discussing how important accountability is in driving the success of a business. While there may be outliers (as there often are when we're talking about humans), I have yet to meet a founder who is capable of working toward and achieving a goal without a structure of accountability. Our natural human tendency is almost always to lose motivation, to drift off, to procrastinate, and ultimately, to lose sight of an end goal. This tendency is why a system of accountability is so important.

How you find that accountability can vary greatly depending on who you are and how you have structured your business. Many entrepreneurs are working as sole proprietors, the sole person in charge of the success of that business. In this case, your accountability partner could be a close friend or relative who has seen you through from the start and who understands your goals and what it will take to achieve them.

I do want to add a little aside that a spouse is often a terrible accountability partner. Often, a spouse is the person who is most invested in the success of the company (aside from the founder) and thus is someone who could become too stressed out by the daily ups and downs of working toward a goal. That said, I don't want to say *never* have your spouse as your accountability partner, but instead, if you do, make sure to build in little emotional checkpoints to make sure the accountability isn't making your spouse overly stressed or anxious over the process.

In larger businesses—ones with multiple employees—daily or weekly scrum meetings or check-in meetings often serve as accountability. They give workers the opportunity to explain what they have worked on, how they have worked, and what progress they have made toward a goal.

Mastermind groups are perhaps what I would consider the best accountability systems for founders and entrepreneurs. Mastermind groups most often consist of three to eight individuals who meet on a regular basis—either virtually or in person—to discuss each person's business and progress in a meaningful and intentional way. Mastermind groups are formed of like-minded entrepreneurs who are invested in each other's stories, but are not impacted by the end results. Basically, they can offer unbiased ideas and thoughts, without getting stressed over the details or failures.

If you are interested in a mastermind group, spend some time researching groups that have already been established in your area and see if you can find one that's open. Shameless plug: ZenFounder offers a variety of groups for entrepreneurs that are often the launching point of meaningful, long-standing masterminds and friendships. If you aren't able to find one, I encourage you to start one yourself. Go to a conference and invite people to join a group after you've had a good conversation. Seek out a few of your entrepreneurial buddies and start meeting for shared accountability and growth.

DEEP RELATIONSHIPS BRING MUTUAL HEALTH

One of the foundational assumptions of my work is that our well-being is contingent on having healthy, deep relationships. Our bodies need physical touch; our minds crave language; our hearts are delighted when we are loved by someone; our souls thrive when we are able to help others. We are a social species. Human development and health is based on connection to other people—first our caregivers, then our friends and a partner, and perhaps our children. These relationships bring comfort and companionship, but also, the people in our lives can serve as sounding boards as we solve problems; escape routes when we need to get away; unifiers when we are struggling to connect; humor when we need a fresh perspective; and the foundation on which we build our businesses, our families, and our goals.

You don't need a lot of friends. You don't need to be an extrovert or a master networker. But you do need three people who will visit you in the hospital or bring you a sandwich in the midst of a tragedy. You need a few people with whom your life is intertwined.

I will go so far as to say that it is impossible to be successful in business or life, and it is impossible to be healthy, without meaningful, deep relationships. People have to be the first thing we invest in, and our priority over other tasks.

On Endings

I want to end this book with the following truth: For an entrepreneur, there are no endings. When you are an entrepreneur, there is no last chapter to write, no tie-breaking buzzer beater at the end of the game, no gallery show that ends with a champagne toast and a shouted "au revoir!" There is no "I have reached the ultimate success" moment when you hang up your old MacBook Pro and retire to the golf course.

Don't get me wrong: There can (and should) be plenty of these moments along the way. I hope your business will take you through many last chapters, many game-ending buzzer beaters, many champagne toasts, and hopefully many hours spent in the sunshine on Hole 9—but I also hope that none of these moments are the end. Because those core values of freedom, ingenuity, adventure, and meaning are values that go far beyond a so-called success metric. Instead, they will push you to grow your business, to keep working, to keep striving, to keep arriving.

This is playing long ball.

Rob was very successful in his business ventures pretty early in his career. Had his entire end goal been to make enough money to support his family, he would have had that moment of arrival about 10 years ago. His technology products were selling well on their own, and he had enough income to sustain our family. If all his career goals were based on that success metric, his co-workers would have bought him a big cake from Costco, toasted his retirement, and he would have spent the rest of his life doing... I don't know what.

Thankfully, Rob is an entrepreneur at heart and has an innate drive to work on something more interesting and more challenging, to learn, to grow, and to create. I love this about him—it's what makes him who he is and what makes his businesses so great. So, even when he had arrived at the point that many would consider "the ultimate success" point, he knew that he wasn't done yet.

Notice I started the last paragraph with the word thankfully. I am grateful that Rob needs more than just a moment of arrival—it is that spirit and that drive that turns the whole wheel of enterprise in our country. Without entrepreneurs who are pushing beyond arrival, who are continuing to create and strive for more, who want to go beyond what anyone thought could be done and create what no one could have imagined creating, our world would be stagnant.

Imagine if Henry Ford had stopped after he created the Model T.

Or if Warren Buffett had decided that after he made his first million, he would just hole up in his house and watch soaps all day.

Instead, both of them relentlessly stepped forward, not toward an end goal or a single point of arrival, but toward a long ball vision, a vision that was much bigger than a single product, a single goal, or a single moment of success.

I mentioned both Ford and Buffett not because they are the only or best entrepreneurs who have ever lived, but instead because both are relentless executors.

In Buffett's book *The Snowball,* he talks about how he saved a small amount of money as a child and refused to spend a cent; he continued to invest that money over and over, saving and reinvesting, until he had built a fortune. Buffett has a knack for money—for saving and earning—so he relentlessly executes on that strength over and over and in effect, creates a snowball.

This is something Rob and I do, too.

We don't count on that lottery ticket, that one moment of arrival, but instead, we relentlessly execute day in and day out knowing that each day is another step toward the next iteration of our life. This is playing long ball. It's the perspective of career and self as a journey—something that is unfolding over time. It's finding what you're good at and finding what you love and being able to do that over a long period of time.

My version of relentless execution is different than Rob's or Ford's or Buffett's. I'm more of a fluid executer—I want to connect with people, to find meaning, to help people become stronger and more in tune with themselves. I continuously (and perhaps relentlessly) execute on that goal, but I do a lot less hammering out products and a lot more showing up and being present.

This is where I want to end this book—not on endings, but on beginnings. On new ideas, on pushing forward, on going beyond the place that you once believed was the end, and making it yet another starting point. That is how you know that you have arrived—when you just hop back onto the path and start working toward the next arrival, the next moment.

Because the journey of arrival is how great businesses are made.

And that is how a free, adventurous, creative, and meaningful life is lived.

Dear Reader,

First, I want to say thank you. This book has been a long-strived-for, long-hoped-for challenge for me. My life's work is helping entrepreneurs like you to lead a life that is successful from a business standpoint, but also full of healthy relationships, meaningful experiences, and long-lasting fulfillment.

The entrepreneurial world is composed of lots of different kinds of folks. Throughout this book, we did our best to use examples, and language, that is inclusive of the many diverse individuals who identify as entrepreneurs. To this end, we alternated male and female pronouns with each chapter. We're always talking about men and women, but the he/she, her/him use of both pronouns gets laborious to read.

Similarly, we used the word "business" to encompass the many different creative and technical pursuits that entrepreneurs have. Perhaps you are an author writing a book, or a coder developing software, or an artist creating beautiful paintings to hang on the walls of our homes. These are all businesses in their own right, and we hope that you can substitute the word business in this book for whatever it is that you have worked so hard to create.

I'd love to connect with you more. Please head over to our free podcast at ZenFounder.com. There, you'll be able to listen more in-depth to many of the topics covered in this book and hear Rob and I riff on the many stories that we hear from founders every day. You can also sign up for our mailing list and learn about events we are attending and where we are speaking.

And we're available to you. Whether you need a few one-on-one consultations to strategize personal burnout prevention, or you'd like the ZenFounder team to host your team retreat or train your executive leadership in how to support the mental wellness of your team. We're here. It is our privilege to work with founders like you.

With gratitude,
Sherry (and Rob) Walling

References

Chapter 2
Center for Disease Control and Prevention. (2016, June 14). Retrieved November 17, 2017, from https://www.cdc.gov/violenceprevention/ acestudy/about.html

Chapter 3
Dweck, C. S. (2016). *Mindset: the new psychology of success.* New York: Ballantine.

Chapter 4
Emmons, R. A. (2007). *Thanks!: how the new science of gratitude can make you happier.* Boston: Houghton Mifflin Co.

Chapter 5
Dahl, M. S., Nielsen, J., & Mojtabai, R. (2010). The effects of becoming an entrepreneur on the use of psychotropics among entrepreneurs and their spouses. *Scandinavian Journal of Public Health, 38*(8), 857-863. doi:10.1177/1403494810375490

Freeman, M. A., Johnson, S. L., Staudenmaier, P. J., & Zisser, M. (2015). *Are Entrepreneurs "Touched with Fire"?* Manuscript in preparation, University of California, San Francisco. http://www.michaelafreemanmd.com/Research_files/

Hecht, J. M. (2015). *Stay: a history of suicide and the philosophies against it.* New Haven: Yale University Press.

Chapter 6
Lipman, V. (2015, July 28). How Important Is Flexible Work? 43% Choose It Over Pay Raise. Retrieved November 17, 2017, from https:// www.forbes.com/sites/victorlipman/2014/10/03/how-important-is-flexible-work-43-choose-it-over-pay-raise/#43e6decd1bb4

Chapter 7

Goleman, D. (2012, March 29). The Sweet Spot for Achievement. Retrieved November 17, 2017, from https://www.psychology-today.com/blog/the-brain-and-emotional-intelligence/201203/the-sweet-spot-achievement

Walling, S. (2015). The ZenFounder Guide to Founder Retreats. https://gumroad.com/l/retreats

Chapter 8

Bailey, C. (2017). *The productivity project: accomplishing more by managing your time, attention, and energy better.* Toronto: Vintage Canada.

Newport, C. (2018). *DEEP WORK: rules for focused success in a distracted world.* S.l.: Grand Central Pub.

Summary of research study on the benefits of yoga: http://www.trauma-center.org/clients/yoga_articles.php

Sharma, A., Madaan, V., & Petty, F. D. (2006). Exercise for Mental Health. Retrieved November 17, 2017, from https://www.ncbi.nlm.nih.gov/pmc/articles/PMC1470658/

Chapter 9

Gallup, I. (2014, October 23). Why So Many New Companies Fail During Their First Five Years. Retrieved November 17, 2017, from http://news.gallup.com/businessjournal/178787/why-new-companies-fail-during-first-five-years.aspx

"Burnout Leaves its Mark on the Brain." *Association for Psychological Science,* www.psychologicalscience.org/news/minds-business/burnout-leaves-its-mark-on-the-brain.html.

Toker, S., Melamed, S., Berliner, S., Zeltser, D., & Shapira, I. (2012). Burnout and Risk of Coronary Heart Disease. *Psychosomatic Medicine, 74*(8), 840-847. doi:10.1097/psy.0b013e31826c3174

Chapter 10
Halko, M., Lahti, T., Hytönen, K., & Jääskeläinen, I. P. (2017). Entrepreneurial and parental love-are they the same? *Human Brain Mapping, 38*(6), 2923-2938. doi:10.1002/hbm.23562

58567120R00104

Made in the USA
Columbia, SC
24 May 2019